POTATO

© Bill Laws 2019

Bill Laws has asserted his right to be identified
as the author of this work.

First published in 2019

British Library Cataloguing in Publication Data
A catalogue record for this book is available
from the British Library.

ISBN 978 1 78521 614 5

Library of Congress catalog card no. 2018953071

Published by Haynes Publishing,
Sparkford, Yeovil, Somerset BA22 7JJ, UK
Tel: 01963 440635
Int. tel: +44 1963 440635
Website: www.haynes.com

Haynes North America Inc.
861 Lawrence Drive, Newbury Park,
California 91320, USA

Designed by Richard Parsons
Cover by Mecob

Images supplied by the author or Shutterstock.
Additional images from Getty pp 16, 19, 21, 26, 28, 29, 74, 77,
91, 122, 123, 124; and Alamy pp 77, 117, 119.

Printed and bound in Malaysia

POTATO

ALL YOU NEED TO KNOW IN ONE CONCISE MANUAL

Bill Laws

Contents

Introduction

Most people love potatoes, and why not? Packed with vitamins and minerals – instead of fats and calories – they perfectly accompany just about any dish, but also make a great meal all on their own. Our love affair with the spud has been evolving for around five centuries, after it reached our shores from the Andean highlands of South America. Ever since then, we've been serving it up as piles of buttery mash, scrumptious roasties, salty seaside chips and bags of crunchy crisps.

Nowadays, a dish of fresh new potatoes signals the arrival of spring, and since the potato is as easily grown in a backyard bucket as in a kitchen garden or farmer's field, it's a treat we can all enjoy. Just follow the instructions given here and find out not only how to chose and cultivate your seed potatoes, but how to harvest, store and ultimately eat and drink them.

This book also reveals the secret side of *Solanum tuberosum*, which, feted by artists, celebrated in the playground, and highly commended in times of war, has some unexpected merits. Did you know you can shine shoes, relieve sunburn and even solve the problem of non-biodegradable packaging with a potato? This book is packed with hints, tips, folk wisdom, recipes, advice and, most of all, affection for the really quite amazing potato.

Chapter 1
The History of the Potato

From its infancy in the Andes to its coming of age in the kitchen gardens of Europe, the potato has raised civilisations, prevented famines, triggered the Irish diaspora and helped win wars. Artists and craftspeople, games-makers and chefs have all celebrated its versatility.

← Peruvian women sell potatoes at a market on Plaza de la Constitucion in Taray. On offer are some of the estimated 4,000 different varieties of *Solanum tuberosum* to be found in the Andean highlands of Peru, Bolivia and Ecuador.

Earliest Beginnings

The potato began life in South America, thousands of years ago when Andean farmers began building terraced fields in the mountains that stitch together Venezuela, Colombia, Peru, Bolivia, Argentina and Chile. Seen from space, these mountains look like a rumpled scarf left out on a frosty night, but at ground level, the birthplace of our potato is formidable.

The iced summits of the Andes, the world's longest mountain range, trail down the western flank of South America. Most of the land between the mountains and the Pacific coastline is arid and inhospitable, yet the western slopes, sheltered from the elements and watered by glacial streams, have been the home of Andean peoples for thousands of years. The members of these valley communities tamed the llama, domesticated the guinea pig and

⬇ Formidable fields: Peruvian farmers plant potatoes in the mountain's shadow.

improved their beans, maize and potatoes by selection. Potatoes grow in the wild as far north as Colorado, USA, but it was only here in the southern Andes – in modern-day Peru and parts of Bolivia – that anyone thought to cultivate them, selecting and refining each crop so that the potato became both highly prized and profitable.

The process was deliberate and systematic. Driven by a will to survive in the harshest conditions, the Andeans first solved the puzzle of how to turn their brutal landscape into a terrain where they could nurture a young crop through freezing winters, encourage it to flourish, and harvest it at its peak. First, they constructed terraced fields in the mountains, filling the terraces with soil that they carried from the alluvial valleys below and building irrigation channels to funnel away run-off water and minimise the risk of erosion. Next, they learned, presumably

A Potato of Sorts

The US Department of Agriculture estimates that there were once thousands of species of potato growing on the Altiplano of the Andes – different strains thriving at different altitudes.

by a process of trial and error, how to plant and select tubers in order to sustain their communities.

We know that early wild potatoes were, in fact, poisonous. Animals naturally avoided eating them, or when they did also ate the clay soil, which absorbed the toxins and protected the animals from harm. The indigenous Andean people gradually learned to cultivate out the toxic strains, in effect domesticating the potato for human consumption; and select seed that would not carry forward the diseases of the previous season. Finally, they learned how to preserve some of the crop so that they could eat well until the next harvest.

⬆The Inca people carved terraced fields from the rugged slopes of the Andes.

Chuño

With such a cruel and unpredictable mountain climate to contend with, these early communities needed to learn to preserve their precious crops for times when harvests were low, or even non-existent. To do this, the early Andean people, created what we know as *chuño*, which not only enabled them to survive through famine, but also provided a source of income, traded as it was for other essentials, including clay, cloth and maize.

To make *chuño*, the Andeans spread out some of their crop on the terraces, leaving the potatoes in the open overnight to freeze them. In the morning, before sunrise, the farmers would cover the potatoes with straw to stop them scorching in the harsh sun. Then, the potatoes were left to freeze overnight again. Between freezings, the Andean farmers trampled them, squeezing out the moisture and releasing the skins,

which were used for other things. The farmers repeated this process of freezing and trampling until all the moisture was gone and, in effect, the potatoes were freeze-dried. Like this, the potatoes (now *chuño*) could last for years, sustaining locals, livestock and even the Inca armies through periods of scarcity.

Potatoes in Europe

'They [the potatoes] are much used in Ireland and America as bread and may be propagated with advantage to poor people.'

John Worlidge, Systema Agriculturae, *1669*

Whereas the ancient South Americans were happily chomping on their wonderful tubers from ancient times, it wasn't until the Spanish *conquistadores* – herdsmen-turned-adventurers who had quit their homelands in southern Spain and set off for South America – that the potato even became known to the Europeans. It's thought that Francisco Pizarro and his men, who arrived in Peru in 1532, were

⬇ The *turmas de tierra*, or earthy truffles, arrived in Europe in the 1500s.

responsible for bringing the potato to Europe, using it to sustain the sailors on their long voyage home.

In 1537, one party of Spanish soldiers, led by Gonzalo Jiménez de Quesada, were looting native homes in Sorocotá, a village in present-day Colombia, when they stumbled on a sort of larder inside one of the huts. Here, they found maize, beans and what one of Quesada's henchmen called *turmas de tierra*, earthy truffles. Growing in the field, the *turmas* were said to have 'scanty flowers of a dull

purple colour and floury roots'. They were 'of good flavour, a gift very acceptable to Indians and a dainty dish even for Spaniards'. This description of the 'dainty dish' recorded by one of Quesada's men is reckoned to be the first European reference to the potato.

However, despite Quesada's optimism, the potato was not well received. It seems inconceivable that the Europeans could be suspicious of a potato, but they were – for hundreds of years! From Prussia to France and Spain to Britain, the potato was treated as a strange and unconventional vegetable, not really fit for human consumption. In Russia in the 18th century, peasants defied an edict from Tsar Nicolas I that compelled them to grow the potato to save themselves from starvation. By the middle of the 1800s, the Russian peasants rebelled, causing what are known as the potato riots. Half a million of them objected to the potato's presence on their land, digging up fields and destroying crops. The violence got so bad that the authorities called in the troops, who fired at rioters, injuring many. Only under the threat of conscription did the rioters finally stop, and begrudgingly the potato wheedled its way into Russian hearts. Such stories of potato dissent and mistrust are repeated across the continent.

Earth Apples

While the Russians were revolting, elsewhere in Europe authorities were waking up to the potato's virtues: it grew fast and was cheap, so it could feed peasants and livestock even during the times of year when grains were scarce. To prevent famine during the 17th century, European farmers began planting potatoes on fallow land. It seemed a win-win scheme.

Scientific Classification

The first scientific classification of the potato is thought to have been in 1596 when Swiss botanist Gaspard Bauhin noted it as *Solanum tuberosum esculentum*. Of course, it's now known as just plain old *Solanum tuberosum*, and sits in the same botanical family as *Solanum lycopersicum*, the tomato.

↑ *Solanum tuberosum esculentum.*

The Potato in Ireland

'The brave Walter Raleigh
Queen Bess's own knight
Brought here from Virginia
The root of delight.'

So went the 19th-century Irish ballad telling the tale of the potato's arrival on the Emerald Isle. But is it an accurate account of how the potato made it to Ireland?

Sir Francis Drake, a mariner and explorer from Tavistock in Devon, had been commissioned by Queen Elizabeth I to conquer the Spanish colonies, In 1586, he is said to have returned home on his ship, the *Golden Hind*, carrying the potato, which he picked up at Cartagena in Columbia. When the *Golden Hind* berthed at Cork in southern Ireland, Drake left a few of his spuds with Thomas Harriot, the gardener of another British nobleman, Sir Walter Raleigh. Harriot grew them at Raleigh's home, Youghal.

Raleigh's kitchen staff are supposed to have mistaken the fruit for the tuber, sending the bitter green galls to the kitchen instead of the spud. The slightly toxic meal resulted in the staff junking the rest of the crop, only to resurrect it for a second trial when Harriot found a nest of fat tubers bubbling up beneath the soil some months later.

This seems plausible enough, but modern historians doubt the story altogether. Drake certainly knew about the 'white' potato (he had come face to face with the chummy little tuber in Chile during a round-the-world voyage in 1577) and Raleigh, meanwhile, was an enthusiastic promoter of new plants coming out of the Americas. However, the most likely explanation for how the potato landed on the shores of Ireland is that it traded its way into southern Britain across the channel from France and the Netherlands around the same time Drake and Raleigh were involved in the west. It may even be that, as one story has it, the Irish first encountered potatoes when they were washed ashore from the wreckage of the Spanish Armada, which came to grief on the rocks of western Britain in 1588.

←The Rotterdam artist Hendrick Sorgh pictured street vendors in the Netherlands selling potatoes, alongside other vegetables, in *The Vegetable Market,* 1662.

In France, however, the peasantry remained suspicious and reluctant to adopt this odd vegetable even as they went hungry. The French royal household showed a callous disregard for their plight, King Louis XVI's consort, Marie Antoinette, reportedly suggesting: *'Qu'ils mangent de la brioche'* (famously, 'Let them eat cake').

However, one French pharmacist, Antoine-Auguste Parmentier, had a better idea: *'Qu'ils mangent des pomme de terre.'* Let them eat earth apples. Parmentier, who had been imprisoned in Prussia and survived on a diet of potatoes, now campaigned vigorously for its culinary use in France. He traded on royal vanity, persuading the court to adopt the delicate, white potato flower as a *boutonnière* and, aided by his friend Antoine-Alexis Cadet de Vaux, the chief apothecary at the old soldiers' Hôtel des Invalides, arranged a

↑ Potato Gatherers by Camille Pissarro, 1881, a theme the artist returned to again and again.

feast where every dish included potatoes. Since one of America's founding fathers, Benjamin Franklin, was also a guest, the potato was usefully promoted on both sides of the Atlantic.

Parmentier dealt Gallic prejudice its final *coup de grâce* when, in 1770, King Louis permitted him to grow a field of potatoes near Versailles. Guards were posted ostentatiously around the plot to protect the crop while under instruction to ignore any thieving. The security arrangements doubled people's curiosity and, under the cover of darkness, the field was emptied of its spuds.

As if to emphasise the potato's victorious arrival, the fashionable flowers in King Louis' Tuileries Garden were replaced

It's thought that along with the wonderful fertiliser, the trading ships brought a fungus-like pathogen that would devastate potato crops and cause famine across Europe, and especially (and most horrifically) in Ireland. Alternative explanations are that the pathogen came with potatoes on ships from Mexico, but either way, DNA samples of potatoes preserved from 1847 at Kew Gardens seem to show beyond a shadow of a doubt that *P. infestans* was the cause of blight.

By the middle of the 19th century, there were 8 million people living in Ireland, many of them subsistence smallholders totally dependent on their daily potato rations. Then, Irish famers, noticing irregular dark spots on the leaves of their crops, pulled up their tubers to find them mushy and inedible. The disease spread and, between

⬇ Another threat: the Colorado beetle reached Europe from America and wrought havoc in the potato fields.

with a crop of potatoes during the French Revolution in 1793. By the end of the 18th century, the potato had become a diet staple throughout Europe.

Guano and Blight

The potato itself was not the only commodity to come out of its cultivation. Guano, the dried urine of birds living on islands off the coast of Peru, was found to have high levels of nitrogen – a natural fertiliser that could profitably and useably increase potato production. The Peruvians began exporting it, and the Europeans bought it in its shiploads. It was potato magic. What could go wrong?

Phytophthora infestans – more commonly, potato blight – that's what.

Pig and Potato War

On 13 December 1853, an Englishman, Charlie Griffin, landed on the island of San Juan, a few miles off the coast of Vancouver, Canada. He was accompanied by a group of Hawaiian shepherds and 1,300 sheep. From these small beginnings, he built a thriving community known as Belle Vue Farm.

When, in 1859, one of Griffin's animals, a boar, went rooting around his neighbour Lyman Cutlar's potato patch, Cutlar shot the beast to protect his crop. The resulting feud turned into an international incident that later became known as the 'Pig and Potato War' – a confrontation between Britain and the USA in which the USA laid claim to the island as a US territory. By 10 August 1859, some reports claim there were more than 400 US soldiers on San Juan Island, along with more than 2,000 British troops who came across the Atlantic on warships. Only in 1872 did international arbitration conclude that San Juan Island was, in fact, US territory, and the British withdrew the last of their troops.

1845 and around 1852, annihilated not only crops, but about 1 million Irish men, women and children, who became so malnourished they starved to death. An estimated further 2 million Irish fled their homeland and arrived on the shores of America and Australia, diseased and weak, but determined to start again in the new worlds. Ireland – to this day – is still recovering.

⬇ A Catholic priest offers his benediction to migrants waiting to leave their homelands for America, Canada, Australia and New Zealand.

Wartime Potatoes

Some 70 years after the Irish Potato Famine, Britain was facing a food crisis of its own. In 1917, during World War I, the British prime minister, David Lloyd George, warned that there are only 'a few weeks in which to sow … the potatoes'. One provincial newspaper declared a potato 'famine' when shops ran out of spuds.

As an unrationed foodstuff, county education committees sprang into action, buying supplies of seed potatoes for children to plant in the school grounds. (Teachers in rural Herefordshire received 63 tons of them.) One wealthy landowner convinced the local military tribunal not to take his gardener to fight on the Front Line in France because he had 'recently grown eight to ten tons of potatoes'; a 16-year-old lad was fined 5 shillings, plus 10 shillings damages, for vandalising 17 rows of potatoes; and a West Midlands' greengrocer, Elizabeth Wright, was threatened with prison for trying to pass off 'table' potatoes as seed potatoes.

⬆ Farm workers in the Netherlands in 1904. Ten years later, the crop played a vital role in World War I.

⬇ Soldiers from the Seaforth Highlands help lift the crop in France, 1916.

(Seed potatoes were 1½p more expensive.) The potato was becoming as vital as ammunition.

Indeed, 'Every Garden a Munition Plant' declared the US National War Garden Commission once the USA entered the war and its School Garden 'Army' enrolled millions of 9- to 15-year-olds. Even as Germany capitulated in 1918, the former lawns of London's Kew Gardens were yielding a crop of nearly 30 tons of potatoes.

Dig for Victory

When, in 1939, central Europe descended into world war for the second time, the potato once again served on the front line. America's Victory Gardens (including one

⬆ French Zouaves lay down their weapons and peel spuds for a midday meal during World War I.

Archibald Findlay

According to some sources, a Scotsman named Archibald Findlay (1841–1921) was the first to breed a blight-resistant potato, helping to establish the tuber as a stable food source for families and soldiers during World War I. He published a book – *The Potato: Its History and Culture With a Descriptive List of Heirloom Potato Varieties* – on all things spud in 1905.

← Farmhands in central Ohio take a break from harvesting the wheat crop to tuck into coffee and mashed spuds for lunch. During World War II, even the White House lawns were dug up so potatoes and other vegetables could be planted there.

on the President's White House lawns) contributed an estimated 40% of the nation's vegetables, while in Britain, Lord Woolton, the Minister of Agriculture, oversaw teh creation of half a million extra allotments in his Dig for Victory campaign, which saw every school tending its own vegetable patch. The campaign not only produced more food, but also a post-war generation of vegetable gardeners, moulded from wartime pupils tending their 'tators and peas'. The potato may not have won the war, but it played a significant role in the battle for food.

Potato Pete

During World War II, the Ministry of Agriculture ran exhibitions to promote Dig for Victory and organised demonstration vegetable plots. The hero of the tuber patch was Potato Pete, a corn-chewing, umbrella-carrying, cartoon potato, who 'wrote' a book of recipes, featuring mock potato omelettes, mock hamburgers and mock duck, the latter made with mashed potatoes, lentils, beans, sage and onions and shaped like a duck.

Pete also had his own anthem:

'Here's the man who ploughs the fields
Here's the girl who lifts up the yield.
Here's the man who deals with the clamp,
So that millions of jaws can chew and
*   champ.*
That's the story and here's the star,
Potato Pete!
Eat up! Ta ta!'

Potato Insults

The potato can be a term of derision, as in 'couch potato'. Leonard Raven-Hill, a cartoonist for the humorous magazine *Punch*, went one step further when he used it to insult hostile Germany during World War I. In 1917, he pictured a German submarine captain threatening the White Cliffs of Dover with the words *'Gott strafe England!'* ('May God punish England!') Standing on the cliffs, a giant British potato thumbed its nose back at the captain and cried: *'Tuber uber alles!'* ('The potato for ever!')

⬇ London evacuees in 1940 get down and dirty to raise Pembrokeshire earlies during World War II.

Potato Weapons

During World War II, a Mounted Home Guard unit armed themselves with rotten spuds during a training exercise on Dartmoor. The Guard managed to lure their 'attackers' – a squad of soldiers pretending to be invading Germans – into an ambush and pelted them with the potatoes. The war games' referee declared it a victory for the Home Guard. Around the same time, Home Guardsmen in the docklands area of London, who were short of weapons and anticipating an enemy invasion, prepared a stock of home-made grenades: potatoes embedded with razor blades.

Modern Times

In Peru today, the potato continues to be a national treasure, with an international centre all of its own. Carlos Ochoa, a relatively obscure Peruvian geneticist, was the Indiana Jones of the potato.

Until his death in 2008, Ochoa discovered more than 80 wild species of potato and, in doing so, contributed to the largest spud gene bank in the world. Starting in the 1950s, the Peruvian botanist trekked through the Andes in search of tuber gold, on one occasion being accused of spying and another time finding himself pursued by Shining Path rebels. Ochoa was responsible for coming up with some important Peruvian varieties, such as Yungay, and several varieties, including *Solanum ochoanum Lechn*, were named in his honour. His potato treasures are stored at the International Potato Center in Lima, Peru, a scientific institution that maintains a potato gene bank.

⬇ Hidden treasures: Peru provided the world with a potato gene bank.

The potato has come a long way since its humble beginnings on the slopes of the world's longest mountain range, and is now the fourth most important food crop in the world, after corn, wheat and rice; and the most important non-grain crop of all. The global potato picture is changing, and yields have rocketed.

In the Netherlands, where around a quarter of the land is devoted to growing the potato, yields are nine times higher than in Uganda, for example, where most of the crop is still raised by hand and harvests average around 5 tonnes per hectare. However, yields in Asia and the east, where much of the crop was also once raised by hand, have soared as India and China, traditionally rice-eating nations, switch to the potato.

The year 2005 marked a historic moment in the story of the spud: it was the first time the East grew more than the West. China now ranks as the world's largest producer of potatoes, with India second in line. According to the Agricultural Marketing Resource Center in the USA, the potato is that country's most prolifically grown vegetable.

Record-breakers

In 2011, Peter Glazebrook (below, with another prizewinner) presented a record-breaking potato at the Royal Bath & West Show in Somerset. His tuber came in at a whopping 4.98kg. But even that wouldn't have been enough potato for the largest serving of mash in 2015 – almost 1,200kg of it, in East Binghamton, New York.

Potato Wrestling

Steve O'Gratin, the pseudonym of Steve Barone, is the founder of the Mashed Potato Wrestling Federation in the USA, and has won the Mashed Potato Wrestling Championships several times. Contestants wrestle each other in a vat of mashed potato in three two-minute rounds. Any potato left over at the end of the competition is fed to cattle in order to minimise waste.

And we don't just use it to stave off famine or make use of fallow land any more. Potatoes are now so much a part of our lives that they are a pastime as well as a foodstuff – from art, to games, to growing whoppers and cooking potato feasts that aim to break world records.

'51 per cent of people eat potatoes every day'

Times of India, June 2018

The Potato in Art

During World War II, Britain deployed war artists at home and abroad to record, in their own inimitable fashion, every aspect of the fighting.

The images ranged from Paul Nash's sea of wrecked German aircraft, *Totes Meer* ('Dead Sea'), to Eric Ravilious' 1940 watercolour *HMS Glorious in the Arctic*. When Ravilious was killed on active service in Iceland, his place was taken by 40-year-old Thomas Hennell, who would himself die in service in Indonesia. Hennell had already chosen an unusual subject for his wartime work: potato picking. His *Potato Harvest at Ridley* (his father was rector of the Kent village) was one of a series of agricultural scenes. He was not, however, the first artist to focus on the potato harvest.

Vincent van Gogh

In the 1880s, Vincent van Gogh was a troubled man. He had moved away from Paris to Nuenen in the Netherlands, where his father was pastor, and where he became involved in a complicated love affair with an older woman who attempted suicide by swallowing strychnine. Vincent had taken a painterly interest in his father's parishioners, picturing the peasants out in the field where the chill northern wind turned the sails of the windmills that drained the dykes.

Several of his works featured the potato: *Peasant Woman Planting Potatoes*, *Peasant and Peasant Woman Planting Potatoes*, *Still Life with an Earthen Bowl and Potatoes* and *Peasant Woman Peeling Potatoes*. His favourite was *The Potato Eaters*, an oil painting based on a quick sketch that, with faintly comic overtones, depicted a family of five tucking into a tea of spuds under the dim light of an oil lamp.

⬇ *Ploughman with Woman Planting Potatoes*, by Vincent van Gogh, 1884.

Vincent's brother Theo wrote in 1885 asking if he had any saleable paintings from his stay at Nuenen. Vincent suggested *The Potato Eaters*. Theo was not impressed. He judged it too dark, too sombre, too serious. A century later, the picture was rated as one of van Gogh's masterpieces, sufficiently valuable to be stolen by art thieves in 1991. (The painting was later recovered.)

Camille Pissarro

Van Gogh was not alone in turning to the *aardappel* crop for inspiration. In 1884, the Dano-French Impressionist Camille Pissarro had moved his family to Éragny-sur-Epte, a rough little hamlet in Normandy. He described the new home as an Eden, the perfect place to work on a masterpiece

↑ *The Potato Eaters* by Vincent van Gogh, one of a series of works by the artist from his native Netherlands.

of his own, *The Potato Harvest*, depicting four working women, heads wrapped in scarves against the autumn chill, picking spuds into wide baskets. Pissarro was the elder statesman of the Impressionists, highly influential, deeply loyal to the idea of painting *en plein air* – in the open – and permanently broke. A century after his death, one of his works would sell for a record £19.7 million.

Other Potato Painters

The art market aside, works like van Gogh's *Peasants Eating Potatoes* and Pissarro's *The Potato Harvest* were not

Ancient Ceramics

The Moche, a sophisticated South American civilization, predated the Inca by several thousand years. The potato was an integral part of their everyday lives. The Moche occupied the Chicama valley, a desert plain stretching between the Andes and the Pacific Ocean, from about 100 to 700AD. The landscape and climate were severe, yet the Moche flourished, growing corn, beans and potatoes using a network of irrigation canals. They also built pyramids and are thought to have engaged in human sacrifice. Today, we have the internet and Instagram to record our lives, but the Moche had clay; their craftspeople produced an extraordinary array of ceramics portraying every aspect of their social lives, from hunting and farming to sex, war, weaving,

human sacrifice – and more sex. There were ceramic potatoes decorated with monkey heads, figures apparently tattooed with potato 'eyes', clay tubers with multiple heads and potato-like figures with disturbing sacrificial mutilations; in short anything that emphasised the cultural significance of the potato in their lives. Some appeared to be designed for burials and others for domestic use. More than 100,000 of these ceramic artefacts survive, now scattered throughout museums and private collections worldwide. Among those museums are Lima's National Museum of Archaeology, Anthropology and History, the Larco Museum (also in Lima), New York's Metropolitan Museum of Art, and Museo del Prado in Madrid.

← The success of the Moche civilisation was largely due to their cultivation of crops such as potatoes, maize and beans. They celebrated these horticultural achievements with ceramic representations of the plants, the people and their gods: the fanged mouths and staring eyes on this effigy jar, fashioned like corn cobs, were associated with the gods of food and fertility, while its mountain-peak heads represented the spirit world of life-giving rain water.

alone in the celebration of the tuber in art. We also have *The Potato Planters* by Jean-François Millet, and the Canadian–American Ernest Lawson and his *Potato Diggers*. In 1871, an Edinburgh illustrator, William Small, executed an affectionate portrait of *Potato Digging in the Kitchen Garden* while fellow Victorian, Tom Lloyd, produced his own charming picture of potatoes being harvested a decade later. Late-Victorian artist Helen Allingham produced a delightful autumnal painting, also called *Digging Potatoes*, depicting a farmer and a little girl, forks in hand – a gentle reminder that the potato's importance crosses generations and sustains us all.

↑ Jean-François Millet's pastoral *The Potato Planters* of 1861 predated the works of other artists, such as Helen Allingham and Carl Larsson.

Arts and Crafts

While in Paris at the turn of the 20th century, Carl Larsson, a leading member of the Swedish Arts and Crafts Movement (1880–1920), distanced himself from the Impressionists when he painted a far bolder watercolour of digging potatoes. His *Potato Harvest* (1905) depicts a group of women and children collecting spuds, sparkling under the October sunshine. 'Ah, these potatoes!' he later wrote of the painting and its subject, 'With fresh or fried salted herring.'

Potato #345

There is art and there is spud art and sometimes the latter can sell for a lot more than a sack of potatoes. Irishman and professional photographer Kevin Abosch (born 1969) has given his country another perspective on the tuber than that of crippling famine. In January 2016, he sold a photograph of a potato – irregular-shaped, pitted and crusty with soil – for £750,000. The spud photo titled *Potato #345* was a new direction for the photographer, whose portfolio was otherwise devoid of vegetables and more familiar with celebrity, among them Johnny Depp, Sinéad O'Connor and Steven Spielberg.

The Potato in Word and Song

Given the popularity of potatoes, it is not surprising that they should turn up in literature – although, when William Shakespeare has Falstaff declaim 'Let the sky rain potatoes; let it thunder to the tune of Green Sleeves' (*The Merry Wives of Windsor*), he is referring to the sweet potato and its supposed amorous properties. (As it goes, the sweet potato is a root vegetable, rather than a tuber, and not a potato at all.)

But US playwright Tennessee Williams (1911–1983) focused on the spud ('I'm potatoes not yet mashed/I'm a check that ain't been cashed') for his poem,

⬇ Spud fan Tennessee Williams (left) with actor Cornel Wilde (right) at a party in Hollywood in 1950.

Sugar in the Cane, one of his *Blue Mountain Ballads* set to music by his friend Paul Bowles. And W.S. Gilbert (1836–1911), of legendary musical duo Gilbert and Sullivan, came up with the neatest potato rhyme in their 1881 satire, *Patience*:

'Then a sentimental passion for a vegetable fashion must excite your languid spleen, An attachment á la Plato for a bashful young potato, Or a not too French French bean!'

The lyrics of singer Dee Dee Sharp's 1962 gold disc hit, 'Mashed Potato Time', were less inspiring: 'Mashed potato – feel it in your feet now!'. But the rhythms more than made amends and club dance floors were soon crowded with boppers doing their own version of the mashed potato. Fifty years on, those same groovers were more likely to be found relaxing in rocking chairs and listening to the more traditional fare of Irish country singer Farmer Dan's celebratory 'Spud, Spud, Spud': 'Good auld Irish spuds are on everybody's plate'.

It was a sentiment shared by those making their way to the annual An Spud-off Mór – a popular spectacle on the Dingle Peninsula in the far southwest of Ireland,

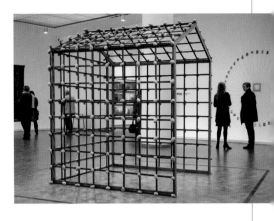

↑ German painter and photographer Sigmar Polke's *Potato House* featuring potatoes mounted on a wooden house-shaped frame.

this inter-parish event centred on the small village of Ballydavid. In a mixture of the serious and the *craic*, champion growers were pitched against local schools, part-time gardeners, and 'spudocrats' (successful potato farmers) to assess plate after plate of tatties. The judges gave serious consideration to the individual merits of each entry, including appearance, texture, taste and ability to satisfy, before declaring the overall winner.

Potato Dancing

Words, music and dance were combined in what must rank as one of the oddest cultural celebrations of the potato of all time in 1944 when the musical number 'Potato Salad' was performed by contortionist dancers Aggie, Maggie and Elmira. Known as the Ross Sisters, they sang in the Metro-Goldwyn-Mayer musical *Broadway Rhythm*: 'Solid potato salad, it's a groovy movie salad, Jack.'

'I've a head like a concertina, I've a tongue like a button-stick, I've a mouth like an old potato, and I'm more than a little sick.'
Rudyard Kipling, 'Cells' from Barrack Room Ballads, 1892

Chapter 2
Growing Potatoes

You don't need an allotment or a large vegetable plot to grow your own potatoes. You can grow them in buckets or large pots. You can cultivate them in a studio apartment. You can even plant up a pot and produce a meal of new potatoes on Christmas Day. Good husbandry – buying reliable seed, for example, and always rotating your crops – will almost guarantee a generous harvest. And, safely stored in a cool, dark place, your potatoes should keep you supplied with tubers until well into the new year.

← A fresh handful of new potatoes straight from the kitchen garden. New potatoes are easy to grow and, because they won't store, should go straight into the cooking pot.

Growing Basics

'The root is of an irregular round shape ... and one digs them up in winter lest they should rot, so full are they of juice.'
Gaspard Bauhin, Phytopinax, *1596*

Every spring, there's a frisson of excitement as gourmets anticipate the arrival of the first earlies: dusky Jersey Royals from the Channel Islands; firm young Noirmoutiers from the French Vendée; soft-skinned Pembroke Earlies from West Wales; nutty Penwith Earlies still streaked with Cornish soil. Harvesting the first garden earlies is, like the arrival of the first swallow in spring, a big day. These baby spuds, ceremonially bathed in butter and served with a spring of mint, make a memorable meal all on their own.

Types and Varieties

Potatoes come in all forms, colours and sizes, from neat little egg-shapes through to mid-sized ovals and kidney-shaped giants bigger than your fist. Growers categorise their potatoes as first earlies, second earlies and maincrop. The first and second earlies, usually served as 'new' or salad potatoes, mature faster – and are planted earlier – than maincrop potatoes, which mature more slowly and produce a bigger crop. A home-grower will lift the maincrop later in the season, for storing.

First and second earlies tend to escape the slug damage and blight that can affect maincrop potatoes later in the summer or early autumn. On the allotment, blight can be more of a problem, as it tends to spread quickly from plot to plot; in private, sheltered gardens, blight can be contained and prove less of a nuisance.

Potato Copyrights

Potato crop yields have increased dramatically over the years. On a farm in the late 1960s, a hectare might produce 19 metric tonnes in a good season. Forty years later, yields had more than doubled to 47 metric tonnes. Bigger yields are almost entirely due to improved selection and, because it can take a decade to develop a new variety, breeders receive the equivalent of a royalty payment on their

seed potatoes. This plant 'copyright', known as Plant Breeders' Rights (PBRs) or Plant Variety Protection, was introduced in the 1970s and lasts 30 years. Potatoes with PBRs may be more expensive than a pallet-load of cut-price 'chitters' on the loss-leaders display at the home-improvement store, but they will almost certainly perform better in your vegetable patch.

The King's Spud

When Queen Victoria's 71-year-old son, Edward VII, took to the throne in 1902, one letter of congratulations came from a loyal subject respectfully requesting that the monarch lend his name to a new potato. In fact, the 'new' King Edward potato was a pretender, having started life many years earlier as a good Northumberland all-rounder, known as the Fellside Hero. The original grower had offloaded his crop to a Manchester dealer. In turn, this dealer hastily shifted on the seed to canny Lincolnshire grower, John Butler. It was Butler who improved the spud and wrote to the royal household, and now takes credit for launching what proved to be one of the longest-reigning British potato varieties.

⬇ Improved varieties mean bigger and better crops in the garden.

A Potato for Your Patch

There are about 250 different varieties of potato available in the UK and suppliers routinely market about 50 of them. Here's a selection with their country of origin and the traits that best recommend them.

First Earlies

Variety	Origin	Characteristics
Arran Pilot	Scotland	Good at fighting off scab and blight; high-yielding.
Casablanca	Scotland	Multi-purpose, smooth-skinned potato for chipping, baking or boiling.
Colleen	Scotland	Light yellow, organic, with good all-round blight resistance.
Duke of York	Scotland	High resistance to scab; excellently flavoured, general-use potato.
Home Guard	Scotland	Strong scab resistance; not a keeper – eat on the day of lifting.
Lady Christl	Netherlands	Versatile enough to serve as a first early or, left in the ground a little longer (11–12 weeks), to produce a second, larger crop. Will rarely flower, so harvest when the foliage is in full flow.
Maris Bard	England	Good general-use potato; good resistance to blight and scab.
Ulster Sceptre	UK	Popular in Ireland; good for baking, boiling, chipping and roasting.
Epicure	UK	Also known as the Ayreshire, recovers quickly from frost; subtle flavour.
Sharpe's Express	UK	Creamy and white; a good candidate for a hyper-early crop.
Vanessa	Netherlands	Pink-red skin; able to survive a dry spring better than most other potatoes.
Pentland Javelin	Scotland	Later developer in earlies' terms, giving a good yield; good general-use potato that performs well in a show tent, too.

↑ Arran Pilot

↑ Duke of York

↑ Pentland Javelin

Top Tatties

Peter Miller is a man who knows his potatoes. He comes from several generations of seedsman and spent more than 50 years as trials manager for Kings Seeds. These are his top tatties by type or use.

- Earlies: Lady Christl and Casablanca
- Second earlies: Nadine and Kestrel
- Maincrop: Cara and Desirée (below)
- Best for salads: Jazzy and Charlotte
- Most disease-tolerant: Setanta
- Exhibitor's favourite: Vales Sovereign
- Best of all? 'I grow Cara as my standby maincrop. It yields well and ticks all the boxes for cooking – roast, jacket, boil and chip. The only slight drawback, it does crop fairly late in the season.'

⬇ Choose a potato variety that works well for you and your garden.

Second Earlies

Variety	Origin	Characteristics
Arran Banner	Scotland	Deep-set eyes and a creamy flesh. Sometimes listed as a maincrop; great for mash.
Estima	Netherlands	Uniform shape and good blight and scab resistance; great kitchen performer – boil, bake or chip.
Jazzy	Netherlands	Small and waxy; good salad potato with the skin on; boil, mash or roast; can produce maincrop if left in the soil.
Catriona	Scotland	Distinctive eyes, which look like they have been touched up with purple eyeliner; big, kidney-shaped, flavoursome all-rounder.
Charlotte	France	Perfect in salads and to roast, skin on; easy to home grow.
Kestrel	Scotland	Tasty and versatile; slug resistant.
Nadine	Scotland	Resistant to most pests and problems; smaller ones are good as new potatoes; larger ones as roasted wedges, or baked.
Wilja	Holland	Good blight and scab resistance; great, floury all-rounder, particularly for boiling, mashing and baking; stores well.

↑ Charlotte

↑ Kestrel

↑ King Edward

↑ Pink Fir Apple

Maincrop

Variety	Origin	Characteristics
Cara	Ireland	Good general worker for baking, boiling and delicious wedges; prefers drier growing conditions; high yields and good blight resistance.
Desirée	Netherlands	Popular, large eater and exhibitor; harvest early in the season for roasting, mashing or use in salads.
Majestic	1911	Will split if left too long in the ground; high and consistent yields.
Maris Piper	UK	Resilient against blight and eelworm; floury, producing perfect triple-cooked chips.
Pentland Crown	Scotland	Good resistance to eelworm and scab; reliable in the ground and the kitchen.
King Edward	UK	Floury texture and creamy flesh, with a distinctive skin blush. Good all-rounder; think quality over quantity for this variety.
Golden Wonder	UK, 1906	It prefers a light soil and plenty of manure and, naturally, makes a decent crisp. A favourite for the craft crisps market.
Pink Fir Apple	France	Bumpy and lumpy – peel after cooking, not before; gives a good nutty flavour.
Setana	Ireland	Drought tolerant and blight resistant; keeps well; its drier flesh is good for roasting and baking.
Vales Sovereign	Scotland	Naturally resistant to disease; yellow flesh and violet-blue flowers.

Sourcing Seed

A seed potato is not a seed: it is a small tuber, specially raised to be grown on.

Home-improvement stores and supermarkets have started to cash in on the seed-potato trade, but usually present the buyer with a woeful choice. Better to look online; send for a seed merchant's mail-order catalogue; or visit a reputable garden centre to make your choice of some of the 50 or so varieties they offer.

One variety may thrive in your soil better than another; there could be a heritage spud worth sampling; or a new variety that is elbowing out competitors on the show bench. Quiz fellow gardeners to find out, join the neighbourhood gardening club, pose questions on social media, or talk to staff at the local garden

⬆ Seed potatoes are ready for planting when they start to sprout.

centre – these experts are usually happy to share their knowledge.

Some gardeners grow their own seed potatoes for the following season, raising a couple of plants in a different part of the garden, isolated from the maincrop, and

⬇ Unlike most other vegetables that are grown from seed, garden spuds are raised from tubers, or 'seed potatoes'.

grown in a clean, disease-free medium, such as a soil-less compost. You can even grow a bowlful of potatoes from old spuds found in the bottom of the vegetable basket, or from those pesky little 'volunteers' (the spuds left over in the ground from last year's crop).

But if you think the do-it-yourself route is for you, beware: potatoes are susceptible to disease, especially blight. They will pass on fungal spores from one generation to the next and infect fresh crops growing nearby. It is almost always better to break the cycle and grow a new crop in fresh ground using fresh, reliable seed potatoes.

↑ Better breeding has improved the potato's resistance to disease.

Yields and Harvest

Buy seed potatoes that are sold loose or have been packed by weight in nets or aerated bags (never buy in plastic bags). As a general guide, 2.5kg (around 20 to 25 potatoes) of first or second earlies seed potatoes should deliver a crop of about 30kg. In a reasonable season, you'll be able to harvest first earlies in 100 days (the first few potatoes teased out of the trench with fingers and thumb). Harvest second earlies after 110 days, and maincrop after 140 days.

Look at the Label

The label on your bag of seed potatoes should tell you:

- the name and origins of the variety
- that it is certified seed (specially grown from virus-free parents)
- whether it's first early, second early or maincrop
- its common characteristics: is it waxy or floury? Good for baking, or chips, or both?

→ A well-labelled seed potato should tell you all you need to know.

Growing Decisions

Growing in the Ground

Potatoes, like any vegetable, will struggle to grow in a cold, wet or shady vegetable plot. Reluctantly, they will tolerate most conditions from heavy clays through to light, sandy soils, but do them a favour: give them a sunny, open site where the soil has been worked to a fine tilth and is rich in nutrients. Your potatoes will be generous in return, especially if the season is frost free.

Growing in Containers

Patio or backyard crops, grown in containers, have the advantage of being moveable – a big gain for growers who live in the far north. You can start a variety such as Sharpe's Express in a frost-free environment, move them outdoors on a

⬆ Yields from container-grown potatoes will be lower than those grown in the garden.

⬇ The potato plants break into flower.

sunny day and pop them back in if the weather forecaster warns of cold weather. Grow earlies in purpose-made potato sacks (avoid standard growing bags used for salads and tomatoes: they are too shallow), redundant plastic compost bins, or even old dustbins, as long as there are holes in the base to provide plenty of drainage.

Good Soil

Britain is blessed with a wide range of soils: there are free-draining sandy soils in parts of East Anglia; heavy clays in some Midlands counties; fertile, but acidic, peaty wetlands in western Scotland, Wales and Ireland; and free-draining and alkaline ground in the chalky Chilterns. Each has its advantages when it comes to potato growing: sandy soils warm more quickly in spring; clays are rich in minerals; peat is a joy to work with. And each has its

Pot Potatoes

A few 15-litre pots are ideal for moveable potato crops. Fill them with soil-less garden-centre compost, or soil from the garden, or a mixture of the two, and provide effective drainage by placing a few broken bricks or plant crocks inside at the bottom of the pot.

downsides: clay and peaty soils can become waterlogged; sandy soils tend to dry out quickly and leach nutrients during watering or heavy rain.

The best soils are those that are rich in humus (natural organic vegetable matter

⬇ A cluster of sack-grown spuds makes the most of a spare space.

made from your compost heap or bought by the bag and usually sold as soil conditioner), worms (two to three to a spadeful of earth), and packed with weeds – if you are able to grow weeds, you can grow spuds.

Of course, we propagators can tweak even the least promising soil so that it produces a healthy crop of spuds. Taken over a new vegetable plot? Dug up that dull lawn in favour of a crop of home-growns? Solve the secrets of the soil by measuring the pH with a home-testing kit. The pH test tells you whether the ground is acid (over 7), alkaline (below 7) or neutral

(7). Readings may vary from one part of the garden to another and if the ground has been limed or fertilised recently, the test will give a biased reading: leave it for six months before retesting.

A healthy pH balance for a normal vegetable garden is between pH5.5 and pH7.5, but potatoes, just to be awkward (and to avoid scab – small rough patches on the skin), prefer slightly acid conditions, closer to pH5–6. Adding well-rotted compost to the soil or layering the compost in the potato trench not only helps the growing spuds, but also does wonders for the seasonal crops that follow.

Earley's Earlies

It's not difficult to grab an early crop of spuds in a naturally heated, frost-resistant, 'cold' frame. Knock your cold frame up out of recycled timber (make it deep enough to shelter the spuds as they grow), line the inner walls with domestic insulation or bubble wrap and cover it with glazed lights or sashes: old window frames are ideal. Now place a 15–20cm layer of stable or farmyard manure at the bottom of the frame, place a 20–30cm layer of fine soil over the top and plant your chitted seed potatoes – Duke of York or Sharpe's Express are good varieties – into the soil, up to 30cm apart.

The appropriately named William Earley described the process in the 1890 edition of *Popular Gardening:* 'A slight hot-bed is made up during the month of January or February. Soil six inches deep is placed thereon. So soon as active growth is observed, all the air possible is given, keeping the temperature at a mean of about 57° [Fahrenheit, or 13°C]. As growth advances fresh soil is

↑ Adopt 19th-century techniques to produce a modern crop of earlies.

added in the form of mouldings-up [and] a full growth will be made superficially until May 20th when, if the crop has not been used, the sashes are entirely removed.'

Find an Allotment

Potato patch too small? Or non-existent? Think about taking on an allotment. Allotments (from the old French to 'share') were originally provided as compensation to landless labourers and their families after the enclosures of the English and Welsh

commons. Supported by the National Society of Allotment and Leisure Gardeners (www.nsalg.org.uk), these companionable communal gardens are as welcoming of amateur gardeners as they are of the horticultural expert. (They are not, however, uncompetitive: expect a race to harvest your first earlies.) Increasingly run by not-for-profit local societies, many offer beginners informal help and support, discounts on seed orders and half plots for starters. Some private landowners let out allotments, as do community organisations such as the local Church of England. To find out about local allotments in your area, talk to your local town, parish, borough or city council or councillor.

↑ Sharing an allotment provides outdoor fun for the whole family.

➜ Low rents and good company make an allotment the sensible option for vegetable growers who lack the space at home.

Planting Out

'Plant late potatoes early and early potatoes late.'
Traditional saying

In much of northern Europe, the first potatoes traditionally went into the ground with a prayer and a blessing on Good Friday, but a warming climate means the first earlies can now go in earlier in March; second earlies mid-March; maincrop mid- to late April. Growing further south, closer to the Gulf Stream, or under horticultural fleece or a cloche allows gardeners the chance to grab even earlier crops.

Prepping and Planting

The most usual way to prepare your seeds for planting is chitting. You can also put the spuds into 10cm-deep trenches in the potato patch; or pop the seeds in a patio sack and leave them to grow under 15cm of growing medium. Or, you can make individual holes in the ground (spaced 30cm apart for first and second earlies, 40cm apart for maincrop, in rows 45cm or 70cm apart, respectively), slip in a single seed potato, back fill the hole and cover the bed with a sheet of horticultural plastic. When you notice the haulms (stalks) pushing up underneath the plastic, cut a hole and let the potato grow on.

⬇ Earlies can be planted more closely together than second earlies or maincrop.

Chitting Your Seeds

The traditional method of starting the potatoes is to chit them, which means sprouting them from the potato seeds. Chitting is not essential, but sprouted tubers will give you a good head start with your potato growing.

1 Collect a few cardboard eggboxes or an egg tray. Place one potato seed in each hollow. (A seed tray would do the job just as well.) Place the filled eggboxes in a cool, frost-free place – a shelf in a garden shed is ideal – and leave them to sprout. Depending on the seed and storage conditions, it should not take more than 10 days for the sprouts to grow.

2 Each eye on the tuber can sprout a green shoot. For a plentiful crop of smaller potatoes, plant the sprouted tubers just as you see them. If you want fewer but larger potatoes, gently pull off most of the side shoots, leaving only the top few, before planting.

⇒ Once the seed potatoes have been planted in the trench, use a hoe or rake to cover them with soil.

← Hang convention and make a hole with a dibber for each seed potato, spreading a little fertiliser around the crop afterwards.

→ The traditional method of ridging a potato crop has the added advantage of creating attractive, almost sculpted beds.

However, with so much plastic waste washing around our oceans, it is time to return to 'trenching and moulding' the potato crop. And besides, nice rows of spuds contribute to the architecture of the vegetable patch, just like rows of runner-bean poles.

If you think your ground may be undernourished, sprinkle around a special potato fertiliser, one high in potassium, on the ground before planting. Then, dig a shallow trench a hand's span (20cm) deep and layer it with well-rotted compost (some gardeners grow a patch of comfrey and

Potato Journal

A garden diary is a thing of delight, a place in which to write down planting times and varieties, and to look back over previous years' yields, successes and failures.

use the leaves as a layer). Cover the compost with a fine dusting of soil and lay the seed potatoes on top before covering them over with 15–20cm of soil. You can slice any large tubers in two, making sure both pieces, or 'cut sets' have a growing eye. (It's best to leave these for a couple of days in a cool, shady place to allow the cut surface to crust over to a cork-like finish. This prevents rot.)

Once you've planted your spuds, mark and label the rows. Write the type and variety on the label and, for good measure, make a note in your garden diary.

New Potatoes at Christmas

Christmas 'earlies', seed potatoes that have been kept in cold store to arrest development, should be bought in summer and planted during July and August. You can grow a suitable variety, such as Nadine, in the greenhouse in containers that you can bring indoors when the weather turns against you, or outdoors in the garden protected by a cloche or fleece. Plant the tubers 30cm apart in rows 12cm deep and 65cm apart. Earth up the plants as usual and cut back the haulms during October. Lift the spuds as and when required.

Care and Cultivation

A potato left exposed on the kitchen windowsill will turn green and inedible. The same greening happens to the growing tuber that pushes out through the soil into the sunlight.

Mounding with a Hoe

To protect your growing potatoes from developing a green tinge, use a draw hoe or a spade to mound the earth up around the growing stalks (also known as haulms). Leave about half the haulms exposed unless there is a risk of frost, in which case you can cover the thrusting tops of the first earlies. Bank up the growing medium around the stems of potatoes you're growing in containers.

⬇ Pulling the earth around the stalks protects the crop and gives it room to grow.

Repeated every week or two, this care strategy will clear weeds, work the soil (the potato crop is a great garden improver) and result in a mounded row, or mould, with 45-degree sides and an umbrella of shading potato leaves. The picture of potato perfection.

Earlies will often manage with little or no watering: too much water will foster leaf growth at the expense of the tuber. But if there is too little rainfall, neither will benefit: watch the crop and if it falls dry for a prolonged period, give the rows a thorough soaking once a fortnight.

Grow to Show

Neighbourhood garden clubs are not only great places to meet other enthusiasts, but they also often host friendly competitions for members. The 'Grow to Show Potato' is a favourite. In late winter, each competitor receives a seed potato. Everyone grows theirs as best they can before the ceremonial autumn weigh-in. The winner is the gardener with the heaviest crop.

For the annual flower and vegetable show, however, judging centres on the all-round qualities of a collection of six potatoes or a 'single dish of five', seen here at the National Vegetable Society Championships at Harrogate Flower Show. Exhibits are usually divided into two classes, kidney or round, although larger shows adopt four classes. Competitors

gain points for condition, size, shape, eyes and uniformity in their potatoes. Speckled or patchy skins, or potatoes that are too big, or have too many eyes or eyes that are deep set, can cost points.

Wipe Away Frost

Spuds will survive the odd touch of frost. Some varieties (Epicure, for example) even recover quickly. One handy tip: if the foliage has been frosted, before the sun comes up, use a cloth to wipe away the ice on the leaves – it is the morning sun that burns frozen leaves, damaging the plant.

The Tattie Bogal

Birds rarely cause a problem with tatties and yet, unlike the Danish *fugleskraemsel*, the French *épouvantail* or the English scarecrow, Scotland's national tattie bogal was given the specific task of protecting the potato crop. A friendly figure, the tattie bogal is closer in character to the scatter-brained Scarecrow, Dorothy's companion in *The Wizard of Oz*, than the sinister figure of Christopher Syn, who roams the marshes in Russell Thorndike's 1915 novel *Doctor Syn*. A host of tattie bogals gather in the far north of Britain each year to grace the Isle of Skye's Tattie Bogal Festival.

➜ Scarecrows have been used to frighten birds away from crops for over 3,000 years.

⬇ The first scarecrows were ancient Egyptian. This modern version on the banks of the River Nile wears Arab dress.

Good Companions

Growing the potato's close Peruvian companions maize (*Zea mays*) and the potato-like oca (*Oxalis tuberosa*) is easy enough. You can start maize (corn on the cob) from seed in small pots in early spring. Germinate the seed under glass or in a plant propagator, harden off the young plants when the risk of frost has passed, and plant them out 30–40cm apart in blocks, rather than lines, to aid cross-fertilisation. Feed, weed and water well through the growing season and harvest when the cob's tassle has dried off. (You can peel back the leaves and take a peep at the cob to check it's ripe.)

The neglected oca in fact makes a sweet and nutty contribution to the salad bowl in winter. Sometimes sold as New Zealand yam, it can be grown like the potato (chit indoors, plant out when the frosts have ceased; raise the tubers only when the foliage has died back in late November and early December), although some gardeners leave it in the ground all year round, diving in for fresh tubers when required.

↑ Hundreds of different varieties of oca are grown in South America.

← The drooping tassels on this stand of sweet corn suggests that the crop is probably ready to harvest.

Harvesting and Storing

It is important not to lift a maincrop too early or leave an early too late. Some varieties of early potatoes are ready for sampling once the flowers start to open. Canny growers and impatient children will nibble away at the row even as the flower buds show.

Give in to the impulse: sacrifice quantity for the quality and take that first handful of pearly coloured baby tubers to the steamer, serving them up at the table with due ceremony.

FIRST EARLIES
Lift these and eat them that day – just as you would green peas – marvelling at how fresh they taste. You can rub away the skins with finger and thumb, or gently scrub them with an abrasive washing-up pad. The tubers require only a gentle scalding or steaming. They can be delicious roasted, too.

⬆ Early potatoes in flower: the crop is nearly ready to be harvested.

⬇ As fresh as they come.

↑ Second earlies will keep a little longer in the vegetable rack.

SECOND EARLIES

You can keep these in the kitchen store for a day or two before eating – any longer and they will start to green over. Again, just use an abrasive pad to rub away the skin, there's no need to reach for a peeler yet.

MAINCROP

The aim of maincrop potatoes is to keep you going through winter. As the potatoes mature, ensure that the tubers are not partly exposed to daylight, and be patient while the haulms turn yellow–brown and wither away in early autumn. Cut down the dead stalks with a knife or sickle and compost them. Give the crop another 10 days or so to mature.

Ready, Steady...

To test maincrop potatoes for readiness, pull out a tuber and rub the skin with your thumb.

- If the skin slides off easily, the crop needs another week or so.
- If the skin isn't budging without a blade, you're good to go.

↑ Allow maincrop potatoes an hour or two in the sun to dry off.

Allotment Workout

Harvest a whole crop in one go and you'll have done more exercise than double the time in the gym. An hour or two of hard graft will see you reap a full crop of winter warmers.

Harvesting Maincrop

Gently fork up the potatoes – a flat-tine fork, rather than the conventional sharp-pronged variety, will cut fewer potatoes and lift the crop. Leave the potatoes laid out behind you as you work the ridge, picking out as many of the marble-sized (and therefore unviable) tubers as you can. (Pop them in a bucket for the compost heap, as left in the ground they will come up as annoying 'volunteers' next season.)

Let the harvest dry in the sun for an hour or two before sorting the spuds into those for storing and those for eating now.

The Dickie Pie

Dickie pie is the traditional Fens' term for the old-fashioned potato clamp – a means to store potatoes outdoors. In a wet winter, you may lose a few more potatoes than you would if the potatoes were stored in a cellar, but if you don't have a cellar and you're short on space, the dickie pie will serve you well.

1 Dig a round trench and line it with a bed of straw or another dry material.
2 Gather up the potatoes you want to store and pile them on the bed, forming them into a pyramid shape.
3 Cover the pyramid with a layer of breathable insulation (again, straw is ideal) to protect the potatoes from the elements, then cover the insulation with a layer of soil.
4 Make a straw 'chimney' at the top to vent the stack.

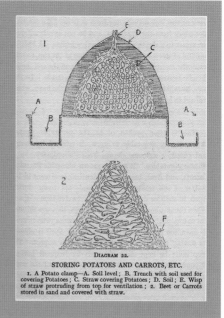

DIAGRAM 22.

STORING POTATOES AND CARROTS, ETC.
1. A Potato clamp—A. Soil level; B. Trench with soil used for covering Potatoes; C. Straw covering Potatoes; D. Soil; E. Wisp of straw protruding from top for ventilation; 2. Beet or Carrots stored in sand and covered with straw.

↑ The dickie pie is a technique for storing potatoes that dates back at least as far as Victorian times.

Place potatoes that have been scraped or pierced in the 'eat soon' basket – depending on the damage, they should keep for a week or two stored in open trays or on a shelf in a cool, dry shed or porch. Also set aside those that have been attacked by slugs or other insects, and any that have caught the daylight and turned green. Once the remainder of the crop is dry and free from extraneous soil (don't wash them until prepping them for a meal), tenderly place them in potato sacks and store them in a cool, dry place, away from strong sunlight. Once you bring them into the kitchen, keep them in a cool place, such as an airy vegetable rack. Don't store uncooked potatoes in the fridge and don't freeze them. In the right conditions, potatoes will store perfectly well for three months or more.

'I'd like something that peels potatoes really quickly – that would be wonderful.'
Terry Jones, British actor, writer, comedian and director in the *Guardian*, December 2010

Troubleshooting

Growing potatoes should be remarkably trouble free. You can avoid the most significant problems – a weakling crop or serious pest attacks – by buying good seed potatoes from a reputable source and rigidly rotating your crops. If problems do occur during the growing season, you have usually two options: rescue what you can, or bin them.

Problem	Possible Causes	Rescue or Bin
No plants	Poor seed, possibly frost damaged.	Start again in a different part of the garden with seed from a reputable supplier.
Plants are pale, weedy and never get going	Planted too early or too late; poor seed or poor land.	Start again in fresh, fertilised ground with certified seed.
Plants grow well, but turn brown almost overnight	A touch of frost.	Plants should recover.
Green foliage starts to become discoloured	Mineral deficiency, a virus or insect attack.	Water, feed and monitor the plants. Look out for insects; take a leaf sample to a friendly garden centre for advice; or take a photo and check it out on social media.

↑ Green foliage starts to become discoloured.

↑ In summer, foliage turns blotchy brown.

Problem	Possible Causes	Rescue or Bin
In summer, foliage turns blotchy brown	Blight is the most serious potato disease there is and can wipe out the crop. However, don't confuse this with the natural die-off of the foliage in the autumn.	If it is blight, remove and destroy the foliage. If the crop is advanced enough, it could be OK. Leave for 10 days before lifting.
Tubers have grey patches, reddish and pulpy underneath	Blight, a tuber disease that causes rotting, has affected the potato.	You'll need to start again, although some tubers may be OK for eating now.
Tubers marked with wrinkled scabs	Potato scab, a tuber disase that causes 'scabs' to form on the potato skin.	Common scab is only skin deep. Peel the spuds before eating and chose a scab-resistant variety next season.
Holes in the tubers	It could be wireworm, particularly common on new ground; slugs; or prolonged wet weather after a dry spell.	Bin the crop and start again.
Stored potatoes turn mushy	It's most likely that one bad tuber is infecting its neighbours.	Sort and restore. It's always good to check your stores periodically and throw out any spuds showing signs of rot.

↑ At this stage, it's not too late to lift the crop.

↑ Too late: blight has killed the potatoes.

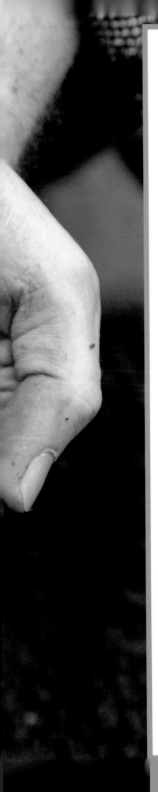

Chapter 3
Home, Health and Well-being

You can clean glass and silverware
with a potato, remove rust and stains
and even keep witches at bay with one.
Solanum tuberosum has been helping
in the household for centuries.

← This heart-shaped little helper has a lot more to offer than
a delicious meal. The utilitarian potato takes pride of
place in kitchen and bathroom cupboards.

Practical Homecare

'Love your parents, have children of your own, bear your fate with acceptance and patience. And relish every mouthful of that salty potato.'
Leo Tolstoy, War and Peace, *1869*

The potato is possibly the most unglamorous and unprepossessing of all the vegetables. At first sight it does not have a lot going for it. It lacks colour, any uniform shape, and, unless cooked in prodigious quantities of fat, has a bland taste. But, do not be fooled: within that knobbly, grubby and blemished exterior lies a veggie with a little bit of magic and some mega-practical applications. It has a breadth of uses that puts it way ahead of other vegetables. The next time you roast your potatoes, or prepare a bowl of chips, do not head for the compost bin with the waste. You can use it, and here's how.

⬇ **Behind that earthy exterior lie some surprising powers.**

Removing Rust

Potatoes contain oxalic acid and this can help dissolve rust. It is so easy and effective, it is a wonder that potatoes are not sold in the supermarket along with other domestic cleaning products.
To tackle light rust:

1 Sprinkle some bicarbonate of soda on a plate.
2 Cut a potato in half and dip the cut side in the bicarbonate of soda. Rub this on the rust.

The oxalic acid in the potato reacts with the bicarbonate of soda to dissolve the hydrated iron oxides. If you have stubborn areas of rust – on pots and pans, for

Bubble Bomb

The association between glass and potatoes extends to the glass-making trade. Glass makers traditionally used a watery potato to reduce the number of tiny seed bubbles in the melt. A potato, thrown into the melt during firing, created a steam bomb that cleared the bubbles.

⬆ Remove rust with potato power ... when combined with a dab of bicarbonate of soda for a chemical reaction.

example – give your potato extra power and dip it in a soapy solution made from washing-up liquid and some warm water, then dip the potato in some bicarbonate of soda and get to work. With a little bit of elbow grease, you will soon have a shiny and sparkling set of pans that look good as new.

Cleaning Glass

Despairing that you never seem to have gleaming, streak-free panes of glass? Want the ultimate solution? Cheaper and often more effective than many branded cleaners, the potato has the answer. Rub a piece of raw potato on the glass and follow up by wiping with a clean cloth. Easy.

⬇ Shining example: the power of a raw potato extends to cleaning glassware and windows, without any harmful checmicals.

Clearing Breakages

Picking up every shard of broken glass from the floor is always a worry – it's always so easy to miss one, and risk lacerating the feet of bare-footed visitors. Cut a potato lengthways (or cut it into a wedge shape to reach the corners between the skirting board and floor) and then rub it on the area where the glass smashed. Any shards of glass will embed themselves in the potato. Dispose of the potato safely afterwards.

Displaying Flowers

Arranging flowers into apparently effortless and natural displays is a challenge to those without florist's fingers. A professional flower arranger will use florist's foam, but this is made using one of the earliest plastics, phenol formaldehyde, much of which gets washed down the sink as fine

debris and eventually out into the oceans. Step forward the potato: it can help you achieve all kinds of floral flights of fancy and is perfectly safe for the environment. Make holes in a potato with a skewer, knitting needle or apple corer, place the potato in the bottom of an opaque vase add the flower stems to the holes and, hey presto, a professional-looking display!

Cleaning Silverware

Tarnished silver can look tired and grubby. The simple solution, with your ever-ready raw potato to hand, is to use it to rub the tarnished items and, like Aladdin rubbing his magic lamp, bring back the shine. Alternatively, rather than discarding the boiling water from a pan of potatoes, keep it for soaking tarnished silverware. Once the potato water has cooled, place the silverware in it for 30 minutes or more.

Cleaning Shoes

With this simple trick you can reclaim the hours you would have lost shoe-shining with a brush and polish. Simply cut a potato in half and rub the cut side on to the shoe. Leave for five minutes, then clean off with a rag. Those brogues will sparkle like never before.

Removing Skin Stains

Beetroot, berries, red cabbage: they all leave an apparently indelible stain on the hands of an unsuspecting cook. The good news is nothing works better than raw potatoes at restoring skin to its natural colour. Rub your skin with the open side of a cut potato for a couple of minutes. Wait another 10 minutes to allow the potato juice to do its work. Finally, rinse your hands well with water, dab them dry with a towel, and what do you have? Clean, stain-free hands.

Magpie's Delight

Bring back the shine to badly corroded coins by inserting them into an old potato and leaving them there for 24 hours. Just take care not to drop them afterwards or the magpies will have them!

↖ A solution to the problem of tarnished silverware: rub the metal with a raw potato or steep the cutlery in a potato solution.

➔ Make a clean start after blackberrying by applying the starchy face of a cut potato.

Traditional Remedies and Customs

Over time and across continents, the potato has played its part in the dark arts, to help and to heal – and to ward away evil (and unwanted lovers).

Deeply Buried

A traditional home remedy for removing warts was to rub the offending wart with a potato and bury the potato. Hey presto, the wart would disappear. And if you were unfortunate enough to live in a neighbourhood plagued by witches, you could bury potatoes at the four corners of your home and keep them at bay. Those who wished to bestow malice on another person had only to carve a reasonable likeness on a potato and bury it with appropriate spells and incantations. If you wanted to achieve a little self-improvement you could identify the characteristic you most despised in yourself and, having marked a potato with a representation of it, bury it.

Elsewhere in the world, the buried potato was not all bad karma. According to Peruvian folklore, interring a potato with a striking resemblance to any human being was considered a sure way to ensure full fertility in the field. The Peruvians viewed 'twin' or co-joined potatoes as being particularly auspicious in this regard.

⬇ Peculiar potato shapes are caused by heat or lack of water rather than evil influences.

Gift to the Gods

One manifestation of the potato's importance in Inca myth and ritual was the gifting of the best of the crop to the gods. The spirit, or *conopas*, which ensured a good crop and protected it from malevolent forces, was known affectionately as *papamama* or Mother Potato. Another type of protection came in the form of *illas*, stone amulets that resembled the figures of animals or plants, including the potato. The *illas* might be carved from the local stone and carried in the sacred coca pouch along with some coca leaves. These amulets were – and still are – regarded as good omens.

A Country Herbal

It took a while for the potato to find a place in the average country herbal, not least because when it was first introduced to Europe it was regarded with deep suspicion and prejudice. During an election in Lewes in 1765, a slogan appeared that read: 'No potatoes. No Popery', suggesting that the innocent tuber was part of some devious Catholic plot against the good Protestants of Sussex. Further north, dour Scottish clergyman advised their parishioners to shun the tuber, for there was, they explained, no mention of the potato in the Bible. Even in the 1760s, when the first edition of the *Encyclopaedia Britannica* was written, its authors described the potato as a 'demonising esculent'.

Most people still had no idea what the plant looked like even though the botanist and herbalist John Gerard (1545–1612) had provided the public with a picture of it 150 years earlier; Gerard published a woodcut showing potato foliage and tubers in his *Herball* in December 1597. On the frontispiece of the book, he was portrayed gazing out at the reader above a coat of arms ('borrowed' from another family) holding a spray of potato foliage in his hands.

Although he claimed his work to be 'the first fruits of these mine own labours', Gerard's 1,484-page *Herball* or *Generall Historie of Plantes* was mostly plagiarised from other works. Yet he provided botanists and the general public with a useful guide to the potato. Having grown the tuber in his garden in Holborn, he was keen to share its virtues: 'The temperature and vertues be referred to the common Potato's, being likewise a food, as also a meat for pleasure, equall in goodnesse and wholesomeness to the same.'

The Tuber of Witches

Curiously, Gerard's successor, Londoner Nicholas Culpeper (1616–54), made no mention of the potato in his *Complete Herbal* of 1653, which suggests that, although the potato had reached England, it was still unknown in parts of London. Even when it did become widespread, people began blaming the poor potato for all manner of ills, from tuberculosis, rickets and syphilis to leprosy and obesity. The potato also suffered (guilt by association maybe) from its close links to the deadly nightshade family, *Solanaceae*. Nightshades contain atropines, a substance not only used to make ointments, but also suspected of having imparted magical powers to witches. Carl Linnaeus (1707–78), whose binominal system for naming plants included classifying the potato as *Solanum tuberosum*, is said to have warned people against eating it because of its association with the nightshades.

← The internet is full of photographs showing our seemingly undying interest in strange-shaped potatoes.

↘ The potato was said to help heartsick and jilted lovers. It was even rumoured to assist expectant mothers.

Potato Blarney

In Ireland, there were all sorts of customs said to help ensure a generous crop. In County Kerry, for example, one tradition was to slip a sprig of cypress in alongside the potatoes on planting day and burn a branch at harvest time. In other parts of Ireland, the priest would sprinkle holy water on the seed potatoes; and potato growers in County Mayo dressed the seed potatoes with a pinch of salt. On 1 February (Brigid's Day), Irish farmers would bring together friends and family to remember the saint, who promised fine weather and fertility in field and home.

In Tipperary, the home of the famous Blarney Stone, new potatoes arrived at the family table accompanied by the blessing: 'May we all be alive and happy this time twelve months.'

Knock at the Door

The traditional Irish practice of fashioning a St Brigid's Cross from rushes on the saint's feast day has its own links with promising a good harvest. A family member bearing the rushes fashioned into a cross, thus representing Saint Brigid, knocks at the door and asks three times to be admitted. The cross is placed symbolically under a pot of potatoes, with the unspoken hope that the harvest will supply enough spuds to feed the family for another year.

Miracle Cures

There are some claims for the magical powers of the potato that need taking with more than the pinch of salt intended to enhance its flavour:

■ Put a potato in your pocket, or thread it on to a string and wear it round your neck to protect against rheumatism.

- Use a peeled potato to cure toothache – keep the potato in a pocket on the same side of your body as the painful tooth and feel the pain abating as the potato decomposes.
- If a nagging cough is your problem, put a slice of raw potato in your sock.

The Lovesick Spud

In the run-up to marriage, spurned lovers could lay a potato skin at their beloved's door to bring about a change of heart. A counter custom from the more remote parts of central Europe, however, suggests that dumping a spud skin on the doorstep of a maiden on 1 May delivered a message of contempt for her. (We suggest that more sound advice to singletons is to eat the potato and get on with your life.) If you do strike it lucky in love and find yourself or your partner pregnant, birthing a big baby is never easy: one folk remedy advocates abstaining from potatoes at night in order to produce a baby with a small head.

'The Indians call this plant Pappus, meaning the roots; by which name also the common Potatoes are called in the Indian countries.'

John Gerard, Herball, *1597*

Medical Matters

Apart from being one of the main and most consumed foods in the world, folklore aside, the spud has several useful medicinal applications.

Tattie Powerhouse

You may think the potato is all starch (20%) and water (80%), but in fact it is a true star in the vegetable world. First, a potato contains only around 164 calories and a whopping 30% of our recommended daily intake of vitamin B6. This vitamin plays an important role in energy metabolism – it breaks down those pesky carbohydrates

Nutrition Facts

Serving size   1 potato (148g/5.2oz)

Amount per serving

Calories   110

	% Daily Value*
Total Fat 0g	0%
Saturated Fat 0g	0%
Trans Fat 0g	
Cholesterol 0mg	0%
Sodium 0mg	0%
Total Carbohydrate 26g	9%
Dietary Fiber 2g	7%
Total Sugars 1g	
Includes 0g Added Sugars	0%
Protein 3g	
Vitamin D 0mcg	0%
Calcium 20mg	2%
Iron 1.1mg	6%
Potassium 620mg	15%
Vitamin C 27mg	30%
Vitamin B$_6$ 0.2mg	10%

* The % Daily Value (DV) tells you how much a nutrient in a sering of food contributes to a daily diet. 2,000 calories a day is used for general nutrition advice.

and proteins into glucose and the amino acids that help cells grow.

And that's not all. The tasty tattie conceals, behind its even tastier skin, a host of minerals: iron, phosphorous, calcium, magnesium and zinc, all helping to build and maintain bone structure and strength. The tuber is an excellent source of vitamin C. (It proved a winner in the battle against scurvy, the disease that afflicted vitamin-C deficient sailors during long sea journeys.) And it is more energy-packed than any other popular vegetable. It even has more potassium than a banana. Finally, it's gluten-free, so those with gluten intolerance or allergy can eat it, too.

Potatoes Against Inflammation

The anti-inflammatory and alkaline content of a tablespoonful of potato juice is thought to have an ameliorating effect on gastric and other digestive problems, such as stomach ulcers. Furthermore, a little potato juice, heated and applied to affected areas can work wonders on joint swelling. (It's also effective for skin complaints and, ahem, haemorrhoids.)

Just Juice

The popular high-street juice bar offers a variety of health-giving veggie drinks, from beetroot juice designed to boost your calcium, iron and intake of vitamins, to plain apple juice, which promises to help the heart and aid digestion. Rarely do they include potato juice. However, potato juice contains all the goodness of a potato, except the fibre (which is in the flesh). To make a tasty potato drink simply juice a clean, peeled potato in a juicer, strain it and add it to your favourite fruit and veg juice.

Against Acid Reflux

Potato juice can provide relief for the discomfort of acid reflux. If you're a sufferer, drink this potato-juice remedy twice a day on an empty stomach. Stop when you feel better.

1 Grab two medium-sized potatoes, wash, clean and – leaving the skin on – cut them into small pieces. (Remove any sprouting or greenish parts.)
2 Using a juicer, extract around 200ml of tattie juice and leave it to settle in the machine for a few minutes to separate the starch residue from the liquid.
3 Pour out the liquid (leaving the residue behind) into a glass and add a little apple or other fruit juice to give it a sweeter kick, then drink.

One home remedy for headaches recommended soaking a potato in vinegar before applying it to the affected temple.

A poultice of raw potato could be the solution to a rash of painful ailments.

Soothing Sunburn

You might want a couple tubers close to hand when you're on holiday. Applied to sunburn, potato juice will have an instant soothing effect. A side effect of too much sun is a migraine or headache: marinate thin slices of potato in vinegar and lay these on your aching temples to reduce the effects.

Easing Stomach Cramps

Whether it is a Maris Piper, Kerr's Pink or your common or garden King Edward, it matters not what sort of potato you pack alongside your swimming costume and insect repellent: they all contain small quantities of atropine, which has an antispasmodic quality, useful in alleviating stomach cramps, often the scourge of the holidaymaker. Eating a raw potato is said to help, but a more digestible alternative is to boil those spuds and eat them plain with no butter.

Relieving Scalds

We instinctively place a burn or scald under cool (not cold) water for several minutes to help minimise pain and reduce swelling. However, a raw potato poultice will also bring relief. Take a peeled, uncooked potato, pound it with a pestle in a mortar and apply the mixture to the affected area.

Odour-free Feet

Smelly feet may constitute more of a social than a medical problem, but it's not nice. Luckily, a potato poultice applied to the feet could be the solution. To make one, finely grate a peeled potato, apply this to the feet, covered with cling film to hold it in place, and leave for 30 minutes before washing off. Alternatively, place slices of raw potatoes in your socks and leave your socks on overnight.

Boosting Libido

The elongated sweet potato (*Ipomoea batatas*), with its beautiful red flesh, has been said to have aphrodisiac qualities. It is rich in beta-carotene and packed with vitamin A, which can help to boost the health of the female reproductive system. It is also packed with potassium, a mineral that is known to counter the effects of salt, helping to lower blood pressure. High blood pressure is linked to a higher risk of erectile dysfunction. You get the picture: just eat lots of them. So, does *Solanum tuberosum* have the same effect on us? Sadly not!

→ Can it restore a flagging libido? Unfortunately not!

Heartening Potatoes

It has been said that over-40s who want to maintain a healthy lifestyle should eat a medium-sized raw potato every day before breakfast to help keep the arteries clear and increase blood flow to the heart. It's a tall order. However, modern research does suggest that potatoes, cooked or uncooked, may play a role in controlling blood pressure. In 2005, scientists at the Institute for Food Research in Norwich identified previously unknown compounds in the potato called kukoamines. These are the same compounds that are present in the bark of a Chinese plant that has been used for centuries to lower blood pressure in traditional Chinese medicine. What's more, every average-sized potato contains about 5g of fibre (found mostly in the skin), which is essential for helping to combat high cholesterol.

The Potato Spa

Being compared to a sack of potatoes is one of life's ultimate insults, but, if you are going to max out on beauty treatments, then you do actually need a sack of potatoes close to hand.

Potato Facial

Few high-end, glitzy beauty salons offer potato facials alongside their microdermabrasions and chemical peels. They could be missing a trick. A spud facemask helps treat acne and other skin conditions, such as dark spots and blemishes. The singer Dolly Parton once said, 'It costs a lot of money to look this cheap.' But, use the potato in your daily beauty regime and, 'It costs next to nothing to look this good.'

Eye puffs

Using rounds of cucumber on tired and puffy eyes is a familiar treatment, but a raw potato is also up to the job. Simply peel a potato and cut it into slices. Wrap a couple of slices in a clean cotton handkerchief and place over the eyes for 20 minutes. Afterwards, wash your refreshed and sparkling eyes with warm water.

Clarify

The age-defining antioxidants in fruit and vegetables are a big sell. The good-old spud can do the job of slowing down the signs of ageing just as well as any expensive vanilla-and-blueberry face mask. Choose an evening when you have no visitors. Peel, boil and mash the potatoes. Allow the mash to cool and then apply it to your face. Leave the potato mask on for 20 minutes, then wash off with cold water.

⬇ A sight for sore eyes when cucumbers are out of season.

⬇ Try using mashed potato for a cool and refreshing facemask.

Exfoliate

Some beauty experts say that we should exfoliate our skin every day. To do this on a budget, grate a potato, apply it to your skin and leave it for 10 minutes, then rinse it off with clean water. This removes dead skin cells and brings new life to tired skin.

➜ Beauty basics: raw grated potato could be the natural remedy, costing virtually nothing, that we're all searching for.

Hair-loss Remedy

Potatoes can cleanse the scalp and unclog hair follicles, helping to prevent hair loss. In addition, potatoes can act as a natural conditioner, adding shine and lustre to the hair. Take 1 tablespoon of potato juice (make your own in a blender or use a store-bought potato juice), mix it with 2 tablespoons of aloe vera juice and 1 tablespoon of honey. Apply to the hair roots and massage into the scalp. Be warned: it is a messy procedure. Cover your hair and leave for a couple of hours, then wash and shampoo your hair. To get the best results, apply the tuber hair conditioner twice a week; you will soon be taken for a close relative of Rapunzel.

Potato Inventions

Never underestimate the little tuber and one of its useful by-products –
starch. Extracted by crushing the tubers, starch is an essential item in
the weaving and dying trade, both as an adhesive sizing agent and as
a coating to strengthen threads used in the weaving of cotton fabrics.

Green Potatoes

Potato starch is also having a significant
impact on the food-packaging industry.
The average UK family unwittingly wastes
around £450 a year on plastic packaging;
meanwhile landfill sites are fit to bursting
and oil wells are emptying fast. It's time to
ditch the plastic for good and find more
sustainable, natural and environmentally
friendly ways to package our shopping.

While a plastic bag containing a takeaway
lunch will take anything between 20 and
100 years to degrade, a substitute made
from potato starch will biodegrade in less
than a month. Even better, the process
we use to manufacture starch-based
packaging produces no noxious fumes
or toxic liquid waste. Look at your
packaging labels: if you are using potato-
starch plates and cutlery at your

← The packaging
industry, and
hopefully the planet,
is benefitting from
the biogradable
potato, and the
search for a solution
to plastic waste.
Although this cup
and set of cultery
looks like plastic,
they are actually
made from potato
starch and can
be composted.

barbecue or wedding party, there is no need for rinsing and recycling afterwards: simply throw them on the compost heap.

The days of mass potato-starch packaging are some way off, but some manufacturers are chipping away at it. New Zealander Richard Williams first found inspiration for his spuddie plates and packaging from Glastonbury Festival of all places. Seems an appropriate place somehow. Festival founder, and dairy farmer, the Pilgrim-bearded Mike Eavis, was fed up with his prize-winning herd suffering no end of stomach problems as a result of his bovine milk producers consuming discarded take-away cups and plates from festival revellers. Exasperated, he asked his old buddy, Richard, to come up with a green solution. And, over the course of 16 years, he did, turning the waste from the potato chip industry into biodegradable packaging. Richard's spud-based wrapping was both microwavable and waterproof. In his 'recipe', Richard mixed the tattie starch with cellulose (the main substance found in plant cell walls, which helps the plant to remain stiff and strong) and water, heated the mix up and then placed it into moulds. Voila! Potato-starch packaging.

Meanwhile, two Herefordshire farmers, Mark Green and Sean Mason, came up with an inspiring idea for their home-made craft crisps in 2018. Not only do they grow their own potatoes and make them into crisps on site, they package them in 100% compostable packets made from eucalyptus pulp, that, they promise, would break down in any domestic compost bin in a matter of a few weeks.

The Skib

The potato itself has been not only the source of great invention, but the inspiration for it, too. In rural Ireland, the wickerwork skib, a large, flat-looking construction with a hole in the middle, had a very practical application as both a colander and a serving dish. At one time, every Irish cottage would have had one, made from any local cane-like materials, such as reed or willow. When the potatoes had finished boiling in a pot on the open fire, the cook would use the skib to drain the potatoes outside, then bring it in, filled with delicious tubers, and use it as a serving dish. After the meal, the basket was rinsed and hung on an outside wall to dry. A new generation of basket makers, inspired by craftspeople such as Irish basket maker Joe Hogan, has revived the fortunes of the traditional skib, which now finds itself decorating apartment walls rather than serving up spuds.

Potato Games

Children in English-speaking countries around the world still enjoy the potato-counting rhyme that will decide who will be 'it':

'One potato, two potatoes,
   three potatoes, four
Five potatoes, six potatoes,
   seven potatoes. More!'

along with the traditional playground rhyme:

'Three potatoes in a pot
Take one out and leave it hot!'

A children's party game called 'Hot Potato' involves sitting in a circle and throwing a potato, or potato-sized object, from person to person while music is played. When it stops, the one holding the potato is out.

In 1949, Brooklyn model maker George Lerner came up with a toy he called Mr Potato Head. The idea flopped initially, seeing as it involved sticking plastic face

Digital Potato Clock

Today, the potato clock is a popular present for budding scientists. Here's how to make one at home:

1 Gather together three potatoes, three 1p coins, three galvanised nails, five pieces of wire connected to small alligator clips at each end, and a 1.5-volt digital clock.
2 Stick each nail and each coin into opposite ends of the three potatoes, leaving just enough metal exposed so you can attach the alligator clips.
3 Wire each potato, nail to coin, in sequence and, having removed the battery from the clock, connect the final nail to the negative (-) terminal on the clock and the coin to the positive (+) terminal. The zinc in the nails and the copper in the coins cause a chemical reaction in the potatoes to produce electricity and power the clock.

← Not a mobile phone in sight: a group of students play the hot potato game in the 1980s. Even in our digital age, the low-tech potato features in traditional counting rhymes like 'one potato, two potatoes'.

parts – ears, noses, eyes, mouths and spectacles – on to real, and at the time not-to-be-wasted potatoes. But Mr Potato Head and his wife struck lucky when they became the first toy to be advertised on television. They were luckier still when, as Mr and Mrs Potato Head, they successfully auditioned for the 1995 film *Toy Story*.

Even earlier, in Russia, children were already enjoying potato play thanks to their copy of the book *Potato Toys*, which was published in 1931. This offered useful instruction on how to create from potatoes a man reading a newspaper with his pet dog beside him, or a traditional Russian samovar complete with teacups.

↑ George Lerner's simple toy struggled to make an impact until it hit the TV screens.

It's Electrifying!

The highest recorded voltage given by a potato battery is 1,224 volts and was achieved by Marie-Therese Gymnasium in Erlangen, Germany, on 7 July 2012. To put that in context, it takes only about 20 volts to power a toy train.

Forget (micro)chips and nuclear power, raw potatoes could be the solution to all our future power supplies. According to *Smithsonian* magazine, just one potato battery could light up a room for a month. Now that really is veggie power...

Chapter 4

Eating and Drinking Potatoes

Of course, the most important thing about the potato is eating it. No number of potato-powered clocks can really change the fact that there's nothing so good in life as a tasty potato recipe. This chapter opens with a few basics on preparing and cooking potatoes, but mostly it is a culinary celebration of the worldwide spud. Once it had circumnavigated the globe from its native Peru, the potato was adopted by chefs from every nation. With the exception of the single-portion fish and chips, the recipes in this chapter are for four people. Ingredients are metric.

← The plain necessities: a bowl of roasted new potatoes taken straight from the garden and flavoured with sprigs of rosemary - the perfect accompaniment to any meal.

Spuds in the Kitchen

'Potatoes: they're not pretty. They're a pain to plant, harvest and sell. But I wouldn't be where I am today without them.'

William Chase, potato farmer, entrepreneur and founder of Tyrrells crisps

A box of spuds, fresh from the garden, is a culinary prize: versatile, storeable, nutritional, gluten-free, fat-free, low in sugar, fine for people with cereal allergy, and a reliable source of fibre and potassium, especially if you value your skins.

New potatoes keep better if they reach the kitchen unwashed, and the fresher they are, the less preparation they need. If the skins have started to set, use a scourer, scrubbing brush or plain (not serrated) knife to scrape them clean. Older potatoes,

if they are to be cooked in the skins, need a more vigorous scrub.

Slice away any blemishes or greening with a knife, although if your potatoes are to be skinned, leave that operation until after peeling. You can cook the spuds in their skins and hand peel them afterwards, while they are still hot. But do you really want to lose that lovely peel? Skins not only give spuds a better taste, they provide fibre and essential vitamins and minerals we all need to stay healthy.

The Gentleman Peeler

How do you peel a spud? Are you a straight or a Y peeler? It seems we all have our peeler of preference. Lancastrians tend towards the single, straight-bladed 'Lancashire', as a sensible alternative to the plain paring knife. Others opt for the swivel-bladed 'Jonas', invented in Sweden in 1953. Six years earlier, however, another Swiss inventor Alfred Neweczerzal came up with the Zena Rex, the iconic Y-shaped potato peeler. The vegetable world was thrown into turmoil.

One of the Zena's most notorious sales pitches came from a Manchester lad, Joe Ades, who had made good in New York City in the 1990s. Dressed in his $1,000 suits, Joe made a name – and an income – for himself selling his $5 Zenas on the streets of Manhattan, where he became known as the Gentleman Peeler.

← This early mechanical potato peeler removes an impressively thin layer of skin.

A Dozen Ways to Prep a Spud

You can boil them and bake them, scrub them and peel them, slice them and dice them. And still they taste good. Here are 12 ways to prep a spud.

1 Grating

Hot or cold, for a dish such as *kartoffelknöedel* or boxty, grating potato is like grating any other vegetable. Use a standard kitchen grater and, if the recipe asks you to keep the starchy liquid, pop the grated potatoes in water in a deep bowl for 10 minutes to let the milky starch settle to the bottom.

2 Chopping

Chop potatoes as if you were slicing cheese. Use the chopping board and a sharp knife to section them. And don't worry about the irregular, rounded edges: it may not be supermarket standard, but it's all good food.

↑ Recipes like *latkes* and rösti call for grated spuds. If you have to squeeze the liquid out, it's a good idea to grate directly on to a clean tea towel or layers of kitchen paper.

3 Chipping

There's something irresistible about ultra-thin chips, what the French celebrate as *pommes julienne* for reasons long forgotten (that particular chipping style has been around for at least 250 years). These fine-cut, wispy matchsticks can be stir-fried with other vegetables, such as celery, onion and carrots. But remember: fatter chips are healthier because they absorb less cooking oil. Opt instead for the traditional English. Slice them thick, leaving the skins on; or section the spud into wedges.

← Fat chips are better for you; they soak up less cooking oil than thin French fries.

4 Boiling

Can cooking potatoes in water really be so difficult? Well, it's worth doing it right – bundling a bag of spuds into a pan, pouring a kettle of hot water over the top and boiling the life out of them while you catch up on social media or do the weekly shop will result in a mushy mess. This is how to boil maincrop potatoes without causing a potato massacre. Cooking them whole retains the flavour and prevents them going mushy.

1 Select potatoes of roughly the same size and scrub them clean. If you are short of time, cut the whole potatoes into same-sized chunks. Place the potatoes in a large pan and cover with cold water. Add a couple of generous pinches of salt.

2 Bring to the boil over a medium–high heat, then reduce the heat and simmer gently with the lid on.

3 Test the potatoes with the point of a sharp paring knife – when they take the point easily, they are cooked. (How long this takes will depend on how big the potatoes were in the first place.)

4 Peel the cooked potatoes if you wish, or eat them with the skins on.

If you're cooking new potatoes, you can drop them straight into boiling water without peeling or chopping, and simmer gently for 8–10 minutes, depending on size. Leave them to stand in the water for 6–10 minutes to finish, then drain.

⬇ Cooking potatoes whole retains flavour and stops them breaking up or going mushy.

5 Blanching

This is an easy way to par-cook your spuds – for example, before roasting, or to remove the skins. Simmer them for 5–10 minutes, depending on their size, in the pan inside a chip basket, if you have one – it makes it easier to lift them out. If roasting, drain well and steam dry before going on to the next stage.

6 Steaming

This is a good way to cook young and old potatoes and, according to many cooks, helps the spud to keep its flavour. Steam earlies fresh from the plot in their skins for 6–10 minutes, depending on size. Maincrop floury potatoes also benefit from steaming in their skins, as they are less likely to fall apart.

↓ Gluten- and fat-free, low in sugar, vegan, non-dairy and fine for anyone with a cereal allergy, potato ticks all the intolerance boxes.

7 Dehydrating Potatoes

Instant dehydrated potatoes enjoyed a market boost in the 1970s and 80s with a series of television adverts featuring clever Martians (with their instant mashed potatoes on board their flying saucer) watching humans struggling to manage without the technology. In the new millennium, we have the means to produce our own home-made instant mash: the food dehydrator.

1 Wash the potatoes and cut out any damaged parts (it's a healthy option to leave the peel on), slice into thin pieces (less than 5cm) or grate, and place immediately in a bowl of water to prevent the potatoes turning brown.

2 Blanch the pieces for 4–6 minutes, then lay them on the shelves of the dehydrator for 8–10 hours at 60°C/ 140°F. They can now be stored in an airtight container until you use them.

3 To rehydrate the potatoes, for hash browns for example, soak them in water for 15 minutes.

Dehydrators can be used to prepare other vegetable chips, fruits and jerky, but they do represent a significant investment. If you do not want to run to the cost of one, place the potatoes on a baking tray lined with baking paper and place them in an oven on the lowest setting for 6–8 hours.

Frying

Twenty people per year die in the UK from accidents involving deep-pan chip fires, and one-fifth of all fires start with a chip pan. It's safer to make oven-roasted chips or use a thermostatic fryer, following the manufacturer's instructions. Another alternative is to shallow-fry using a heavy-based pan, a good-quality oil and turning the potatoes with a fish slice until they are brown all over.

↑ The nation's favourite potato dish can be safely made in the oven.

Frying Safety

When it comes to frying, play safe.

- Dry your home-made chips thoroughly before frying – their water will spit in hot oil.
- Keep a thick fire blanket handy in case of accidents
- Never throw water on burning oil.
- Never fry with children or pets close by.
- Once the oil has cooled down, dispose of it in the compost bin. It should only be used once.

➔ Take great care with hot oil.

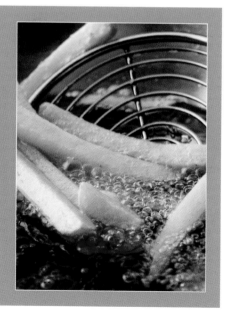

Baking

If the potato can be a focus for meditation, it's worth knowing that it's more Zen to leave the skins on and, having washed and dried your Maris Piper or King Edward, settle down to contemplate the infinite universe while your spuds quietly bake themselves into a complete meal.

Rub a little sea salt and olive oil into the skins before they go on to the baking tray and cut a cross on the top. You can speed up the cooking time (45–60 minutes for a generous-sized spud at 200°C/400°F/Gas 6) by skewering the potatoes or using a potato baking spike. When the outsides are crisp and the insides tender they are done. The best way to serve them is to quickly pinch each side of the cut cross to break open the potato to release the steam; this makes the insides beautifully fluffy. Top with some butter and a sprinkling of salt.

↑ The nation's favourite winter warmer, baked pototo with plenty of butter.

Microwave 'Baking'

You can bake potatoes in a microwave, although zapped bakers will lack the crusty skins of oven bakers – this is more a functional meal in minutes, and far less Zen. Follow the manufacturer's instructions, pricking the skins to prevent them from bursting. Allow 5–6 minutes per potato on high, then let the potatoes stand to ensure they are evenly cooked through. If you just can't bear to not have a crusty skin, but need the microwave timing, you can compromise and three-quarters cook them in the microwave and then finish them off in the oven.

For succulent campfire spuds or barbecues, wrap your potatoes in foil and thrust into the embers. Give them about 50 minutes – the exact time depending on the heat and the size of the potato (you'll need less time if you slit them almost through or adopt the Swedish *Hasselback* method) and eat them drizzled with butter or margarine and your favourite sauce.

Clay-pot cooking (using an unglazed terracotta pot) really enhances the flavours. Soak the pot in cool water for 10 minutes. Put the spuds in the pot with a drop of olive oil, salt, pepper and a few flavourings, such as chopped herbs, onion, garlic or streaky bacon. Don't put the pot straight into a hot over as it may crack. Instead, having popped on the lid, place it in a cold oven and gradually increase the heat. At 200°C/400°F/Gas 6 they should take around 45 minutes.

⬆ Potatoes baked on the campfire – an outdoor treat at any time of the year.

⬇ The thinly sliced tops of *Hasselback* pototoes help absorb the garlic-scented butter.

10 Roasting

Roasting is the safe solution to lovely-tasting, healthy potatoes. And it's so easy. If you want the best results, select a good roasting variety, such as Desirée, King Edward or Maris Piper; blanch or par-boil for 3–5 minutes. Drain and dry thoroughly while the roasting tin, and a little fat or oil, heats in the oven at 220°C/425°F/Gas 7. (Too much fat turns spuds soggy; too little leaves them dry.)

For crispy spuds, rough them up, bumping them around in a colander or hatching the surface with a fork. Pop them straight in the tin with the hot oil or fat and let them roast for 40–50 minutes. Add a sprig of rosemary, a clove of garlic and

⬆ Par-boiling potatoes and giving them a good shake before roasting helps develop crispy edges.

a handful of chopped bacon halfway through to give the roasties a Mediterranean flavour.

Follow the same process for roasting potato wedges. Add your favourite seasoning – curry powder, a couple of garlic cloves, a sprinkle of Parmesan cheese – halfway through the cooking.

⬇ Roast potatoes are made even more irresistable by a few cloves of garlic and sprigs of rosemary half way through cooking.

11 Mashing

There's nothing worse than lumpy mash, and it's a good option for thickening soups and stews. For perfect mashing, you need a floury rather than waxy potato and you'll need to peel. For velvety results, use a hand masher, adding a dash of milk, a knob of butter and seasoning. Finish by whipping the mash to a creamy finish with a wooden spoon. Piping mashed potatoes produces dainty rosettes, which, brushed with a dash of beaten egg and water, should be popped back in the oven on the baking tray and finished to a golden yellow at 190°C/375°F/Gas 5. Similarly, you can pipe your mash into a crusty pie topping, rounding it off under the grill for 5 minutes; or create potato nests, glazed in exactly the same way as the rosettes. Or you can pipe out (or hand form) potato balls or croquettes, for shallow-frying.

⬆ Creamy mash needs a good pumelling for the best results.

⬇ Substitute a proportion of the flour with mashed potato in your favourite pastry recipes.

12 Potato Pastry

Mash can make a distinctive and slightly healthier pastry: just replace half the flour in your recipe with the equivalent amount of mashed potato.

Recipes from around the world
Britain

The average English family eats more potatoes than its native farmers can grow, while almost half of Scotland's home-grown spuds are destined for someone else's farm or garden. Raised for seed rather than 'ware' or household consumption, Scottish seed potatoes are exported as far as China. The number of English potato fields may have shrunk by half since 1960, but Britain still ranks as Number 12 in the growing stakes.

Fish and Chips

The British may not have invented the dish, but we've made it our own, with a fish and chip shop on every high street throughout the UK, from super posh to dead basic. Use a thermostatic or digital air fryer to fry the fish for perfectly crispy results. Serves 1

FOR THE CHIPS
- 225g potatoes (Golden Wonder or Maris Piper), cleaned and scrubbed, skin on
- 2 tbsp olive oil
- salt and vinegar

FOR THE FISH
- 175g cod, haddock or other white skinless, boneless fish fillet, dusted with cornflour
- 200g plain flour
- 300ml beer
- sunflower oil, for deep-frying
- salt and pepper
- mushy peas and lemon wedges, to serve

1. Heat the oven to 200°C/400°F/Gas 6. Chop the potatoes into finger-width chips. Run them under the cold tap and dry with a tea towel.
2. Heat the 2 tablespoons of oil in a shallow baking tray. Place in the oven and allow the oil to heat up for a few minutes.
3. Remove the tray from the oven and add the chips in a single layer. Roast for 45–50 minutes, turning the chips occasionally, so they brown on all sides.
4. About 15–20 minutes before the end of the cooking time, put the flour in a bowl and season it with salt and pepper. Slowly add the beer, whisking to make a smooth batter.
5. Dip the fish in batter to coat, allow the excess to drop off, then place in the fryer and fry, following the manufacturer's instructions, until golden.
6. Remove from the fryer, set aside on kitchen paper and keep warm until the chips are ready, then transfer to a plate and serve with a spoonful of mushy peas, a wedge of lemon and the piping-hot chips alongside.

Chippy History

There have been rival claims over which location, in the 1860s, hosted the first British chippy. Rival contenders include northerner John Lees and his fish and chip hut near Mossley market in Lancashire and stallholder Jo Malin in London's East End, which advertised fish 'fried in the Jewish fashion'. Although this suggests that it was the Jewish community who gave us their traditional fried fish, most coastal fishing communities tucked into fried fish and tatties long before the chippie arrived on our high streets.

It was the burgeoning railways that spread the fish and chip habit nationwide and by the 1880s the Manchester, Sheffield and Liverpool Railway Company was shifting around a quarter of the nation's fish out of Grimsby harbour. The rapacious combination of steam locomotive and steam trawler would, however, prove too much for the high seas: overfishing decimated North Sea fish stocks and it would be more than a century before reserves of white fish began to recover.

⬇ Soldiers from the Duke of Wellington's Regiment (West Riding) queue for their fish and chips at Wathgill Camp in 1936 during territorial manoeuvres. During World War II, this was the only dish the British government refused to ration.

Neeps and Tatties

This classic Scottish dish of mashed potatoes and swede is traditionally served as an accompaniment to haggis, and features on Burns Night. You need to cook the swede and potatoes in different pans because swede takes longer to become tender.

YOU WILL NEED

- 500g swede, peeled and diced
- 500g mashing potatoes, such as Pentland Crown or Colleen, peeled and diced
- knob of butter
- salt and pepper

1 Bring a large pan of lightly salted water to the boil and add the swede (neeps), then simmer for 12 minutes.

2 Add in the potatoes (tatties) and boil for another 12–15 minutes, until all the vegetables are tender.

3 Drain, mash, season and let the knob of butter melt on top when you serve to accompany a haggis and some steamed greens.

Scottish Macaroons

Perhaps the only candy in the world made from potatoes, Scottish macaroons were invented by John J. Lees, confectioner, in 1931. Since then, they have become a national classic, and although Lees no longer use potato in their commercial version, the good news is they're really easy to make at home.

YOU WILL NEED

- 1 large potato, boiled and drained (100g cooked)
- 2–3 drops vanilla extract
- 400–500g icing sugar
- 300g dark chocolate
- 100g dessicated (unsweetened) coconut, dry-roasted until golden brown

1   Mash the cooked potato until there are no lumps, then leave until completely cool.
2   Place the mash in a bowl and add the vanilla extract and 100g of the sugar. Mix well. The potato will seem very dry but it will gradually change consistency. Keep adding the icing sugar, 100g at a time, mixing well after each addition, until you have a stiff, white fondant.
3   Line a baking tray with baking parchment, tip the fondant on and press flat. Cover with cling film and freeze for an hour.
4   Remove the fondant from the freezer and cut into little bar shapes. You could also form it into balls if you wish, once it's softened.
5   Melt the chocolate in a heatproof bowl above a pan of simmering water, or in the microwave for a few seconds. Place the coconut on a plate.
6   Dip the fondant bars first in chocolate, then roll in toasted coconut and place on to baking parchment to set.

Robert Burns

'Curse Thou his basket and his store
Kail an' potatoes'
Holy Willie's Prayer, Robert Burns

Born in 1795 in Ayreshire, Robert Burns was

sometimes portrayed as a mawkish, 'ploughman poet'. Yet his wit was as razor sharp as his satirical attack on religious hypocrisy in Holy Willie's Prayer. Burns Night falls on 25 January, the day of his birth.

Cawl

As unique as champagne and Parma ham, Pembrokeshire Earlies are a regional speciality. This Welsh region, which has been growing its own since the mid-1700s, has a special relationship with the potato. A comforting, soupy winter warmer, cawl tends to combine lamb and leeks, but in hard times when meat was too expensive to use every day, it was the *tatws* that made up for it. This is a vegetarian cawl.

YOU WILL NEED

- 1 swede, peeled and cut into large chunks
- 2–3 tsp yeast extract, to taste
- 2 carrots, cut into large chunks
- 2 large potatoes, peeled and cut into large chunks
- 1 large leek, cut into 2cm-thick slices
- 2 parsnips, peeled and cut into large chunks
- salt and pepper

1. Place the swede in a large pan with 1 litre of boiling water and the yeast extract. Simmer for 10–15 minutes over a low heat.
2. Add the carrots and simmer for a further 10–15 minutes, until softened, then add the potatoes, leek and parsnips and cook, covered, for 10–15 minutes, until all the vegetables are tender. Season with salt and pepper.
3. Serve sprinkled with an extra twist of pepper. It is delicious accompanied with warm, buttered bread.

Dyled Tatws

The potato crop offered salvation to country people in the poorer, western parts of the British Isles, including Wales, during the 17th and 18th centuries.

At first, the Welsh were as reluctant as the Russians to embrace their *tatws*, although one pioneering farmer on Anglesey, Edward Wynne (1681–1757), was managing three 'potato gardens' by 1730, growing spuds procured from Ireland. Landless labourers in other parts of Wales who were loaned their own potato gardens were said to owe a *dyled tato*, a potato debt, to the landowner who provided the plots.

One and One

Why should the British request 'chips', the Americans 'French fries', the French ask for '*pommes frites*' (fried apples) and Dubliners demand a 'one and one'? The British chip seems to have risen with the fish and chip shop in the mid-1800s. As for America's French fries, it could have been US president Thomas Jefferson who implied that fries were French after dining on potatoes 'served in the French manner' in 1802. (Jefferson had shared a meal with the great French exponent of the potatoes, Auguste Parmentier, during his stay in Paris.)

While most of us now accept that thin-cut 'chips' should properly be ordered as French fries, the French still dispute circumstantial evidence suggesting they nicked their idea from the Belgians. Meanwhile, Dubliners like to tuck into their 'one and one' after Italians Giuseppe and Palma Cervi started selling fried fish and tatties from a market stall in Great Brunswick Street in the 1880s. '*Uno di questa? Uno di quella?*' ('One of this? One of that?') Palma would ask her customers. 'I'll have a one and a one', came the answer.

Punchnep

This is a winter comfort food, perfect with roasts or grills. As with its Scottish counterpart, neeps and tatties, punchnep marries two root vegetables for a lighter and more nutritious dish.

YOU WILL NEED
- 500g good mashing potatoes, such as Arran Banner or Catriona
- 500g white turnips
- 50g butter, or to taste
- salt and pepper
- 150ml single cream, to serve

1 Peel and cook the potatoes and turnips in two separate pans (the turnips usually take longer).
2 Drain the vegetables and mash. Add 25g butter to each mash, then combine the two.
3 Season with salt and pepper, then slip the mash into a nice dish, smooth the top and punch divots in it with the handle of a wooden spoon. Warm the cream and use a jug to drizzle it into the holes before serving.

Potato Puffs

These delicious fluffy side dishes go well with a green salad, but originally must have been a way to make a little meat go a long way.

YOU WILL NEED

- 280g mashed, cooled potatoes, such as Desirée or Arran Banner
- 250g plain flour
- 225g minced cold meat or spicy lentils, for the filling
- vegetable oil, for frying
- green salad, to serve

1. Mix together the mash and the flour, then tip out on to a lightly floured surface and roll out to 5mm thick.
2. Divide the potato dough into four equal portions and roll each out to a square roughly 12x12cm. Place one-quarter of the filling in the centre of each square.
3. With lightly floured hands, fold over each square to enclose the filling, then press the edges together to seal.
4. Heat a little vegetable oil in a large frying pan to coat the base. Add the potato puffs (fry in batches, if necessary) and cook over a low heat, turning occasionally, until the puffs are light brown on all sides.
5. Bake for 10 minutes in a hot oven to make sure the puffs are heated all the way through. Transfer to plates and serve hot with a fresh green salad.

Recipes from around the world
Denmark

The Danes like to combine their traditional meat and fish dishes with the new style of healthier Danish cooking, with an emphasis on wild, home-raised products.

Potato Salad

Kold kartoffelsalat is a classic companion to everything that goes on to the grill in summer, but it's also perfect with smoked salmon and rye bread or cold cuts like ham, pancetta and pastrami.

YOU WILL NEED

- 650g potatoes
- 200ml sour cream
- 200ml plain yogurt
- 1 red onion, finely chopped, optional
- 100ml finely chopped fresh chives
- salt and pepper

1 Peel the potatoes, cut into bite-sized chunks, then boil them in salted water for 10–15 minutes. Don't overcook them.

2 As the potatoes cook, combine the sour cream, yogurt and onion, if using, in a bowl with the chives and salt and pepper.

3 Allow the potatoes to cool a little before adding them to the mix.

4 There are limitless variations of the basic recipe, which involve adding any of the following: mayonnaise, fromage frais, Dijon mustard, curry powder, a dash of cider vinegar, sliced apple, gerkins or sliced radish.

Recipes from around the world
Eastern Europe

Once they settled their differences over the 'foreign' potato, countries from Romania to Russia settled down to cultivate and cook the vegetable that was to become key to their cuisines.

Latkes

Originally, the Yiddish *latkes* were made from cheese, but this is a delicious potato version.

YOU WILL NEED

- 2 large potatoes, such as Maris Piper or King Edward, peeled and grated
- 1 onion, grated
- 1 egg, beaten
- 2 tbsp matzo meal (finely crushed matzo crackers)
- vegetable oil
- salt and pepper
- sour cream or apple sauce, to serve

1. Place the potato and onion in a tea towel or colander and squeeze out the moisture, as with the recipe for boxty (see page 108).
2. Place the vegetables in a mixing bowl, add the egg and matzo meal, season, and mix well.
3. Heat a little oil in a heavy-based pan. Add small spoonfuls of the mixture to the hot oil – if they do not sizzle, the oil is not hot enough.
4. Flatten out the *latkes* with the back of the spoon and turn them to cook on both sides, until golden brown and set.
5. Lift out the *latkes*, drain them on kitchen paper and serve with sour cream or apple sauce.

Knish

A popular street food, these Jewish baked-potato dumplings from eastern and central Europe were taken to the USA in the early 1900s where they have enjoyed a recent, millennial revival.

YOU WILL NEED
- 2 tbsp vegetable oil
- 3 large onions, finely chopped
- 550g potatoes, such as Wilja, peeled, cooked, mashed and cooled
- 1 egg
- sprig of parsley
- salt and pepper

FOR THE DOUGH
- 2 large eggs
- 120ml vegetable oil, plus extra for brushing
- 1 tbsp white vinegar
- ½ tsp salt
- 500g plain flour

1 For the dough, beat the eggs and set aside a little for glazing the pastry. Mix the remaining egg with the oil, vinegar, 250ml water and the salt, then add the flour. Knead the mixture to a smooth dough.
2 Shape into a ball, cover with a damp cloth or cling film and place in the fridge to rest for 30 minutes.
3 Meanwhile, heat the oil in a frying pan over a medium heat and add the onion. Fry until golden brown, then set aside to cool.
4 In a large bowl, mix potatoes with the egg and parsley and add the cooled onion. Season with salt and pepper.
5 Divide the dough into four and roll each piece into thin, flat rectangles; dust with flour and place between two sheets of waxed paper. Rest the dough sheets for 15 minutes.
6 Heat the oven to 190°C/375°F/Gas 5.
7 Stretch the rectangles as thin as possible. Leaving a 2.5cm border, spread a quarter of the filling in a log shape across each sheet of dough, about 5cm thick, and roll them up.
8 Seal the open ends with a brush of oil and place on a baking tray lined with baking paper, seam side down. Brush the rolls with the remaining egg mixed with a little water. Bake for 25–30 minutes, until golden brown.
9 When baked, divide into *knishes* by cutting 5cm diagonals. If you wish, the rolls can be cut into *knishes* once cooled, and then heated up for 10 minutes before being served.

Recipes from around the world
France

Addicted to classic varieties, such as the 150-year-old waxy, yellow-skinned Belle de Fontenay and that stalwart all rounder, Charlotte, French cooks traditionally made the most of their *pommes de terre*.

Dauphinoise

Derived from the French *dauphin* – the Count of Duphiné wore an emblematic *dauphin* or dolphin on his coat of arms – this rich dish is a simple fusion of floury potatoes, garlic and double cream.

YOU WILL NEED

- ½ garlic clove
- 1 tbsp salted butter, for greasing
- 675g floury potatoes, such as King Edward or Wilja, peeled and very thinly sliced
- 300ml double cream
- salt and pepper

1. Heat the oven to 180°C/350°F/Gas 4.
2. Rub around the sides of a shallow ovenproof dish with the cut side of the garlic clove, then grease generously with half of the butter.
3. Layer the potatoes in the dish, seasoning each layer with a little salt and pepper.
4. When all the potato slices are in the dish, pour the cream over and season again with salt and pepper. Dot the remaining butter over the top.
5. Cover with foil and bake for approximately 1½ hours, or until the potatoes are cooked through and tender.
6. Remove the foil and bake, uncovered, for another 30 minutes, until the top is golden and all the liquid has been absorbed.

Lyonnaise

A French dish from the city of Lyon, thinly sliced potatoes are par-boiled, then fried in butter with onion, and served with a sprinkling of fresh parsley.

YOU WILL NEED

- 850g potatoes, peeled and cut into 1cm-thick slices
- 3 tbsp olive oil
- large knob of butter
- 2 onions, sliced
- 2 garlic cloves, crushed
- salt and pepper
- chopped parsley, to serve

1 Put the spuds in a pan of slightly salted water, bring to the boil and simmer until tender, but not falling apart (about 2 minutes). Drain well.

2 Heat the oil and butter in a frying pan over a medium heat, then add the onions and garlic and fry until softened but not browned.

3 Add the potatoes and season with salt and pepper. Cook until they begin to brown nicely, turning the slices regularly so that they brown on both sides.

4 Transfer to a warmed serving dish, sprinkle with parsley and serve.

Parmentier

Monsieur Parmentier persuaded his countrymen to adopt the potato, and introduced US President Thomas Jefferson to 'French' fries. The French responded by naming this dish in his honour.

YOU WILL NEED

- 800g potatoes, cut into thumbnail-sized chunks
- 2 tbsp vegetable oil
- 1 onion, sliced
- 2 garlic cloves, crushed
- 1 shallot, diced
- sprig of rosemary
- pinch of thyme
- salt and pepper

1. Heat the oven to 220°C/425°F/Gas 7. Place the potato chunks in a bowl of water to soak for 30 minutes.
2. Pour the oil into a shallow baking dish and pop it in the oven to heat up.
3. Drain the potatoes and dry them well, then add them to the baking dish along with the other ingredients. Stir with a wooden spoon to coat the potatoes evenly in the hot oil.
4. Bake for 40–45 minutes, until golden brown. Serve immediately.

Vichyssoise

A cold soup for a hot day, Vichyssoise takes its name from the spa town in central France.

YOU WILL NEED

- 1 tbsp olive oil
- 3 leeks, sliced thinly
- 350g potatoes, peeled and cut into small chunks
- 600ml vegetable stock
- 1 bay leaf
- 175g watercress, plus a little extra to garnish
- 175ml single cream
- salt and pepper

1. Heat the oil is a large pan over a medium heat. Add the leeks and cook for about 10 minutes, to soften.
2. Add the potatoes, stock, 450ml water and the bay leaf, and bring to the boil. Lower the heat and simmer, covered, until the potatoes are cooked (about 10 minutes).
3. Remove the bay leaf, add the watercress and simmer to wilt, then remove the pan from the heat. Stir in the salt and pepper.
4. Allow the soup to cool a little, then use a stick blender to blend it to a smooth consistency. Stir in half the cream and transfer to a bowl. Cover and leave until cold, then place in the fridge to chill completely.
5. Serve cold, with a swirl of the remaining cream stirred into each bowl and garnished with a little watercress.

Recipes from around the world
Germany

Germany is wedded to its spuds with *Salzkartoffeln* (potatoes boiled in salted water), *Kartoffelbrei* (mashed potato), *Fritten* (fries) and *Schupfnudel* (a version of gnocchi) made with potatoes.

Kartoffelknöedel

Similar to the Swedish *kroppkakor*, the potato dumpling uses raw and mashed potato. This is the basic recipe, but you can fill them with a little sauerkraut or ham – placing the meat into the centre of the dumpling and moulding around it – if you like.

1 Measure out 300g of the potatoes, place them in a pan of salted boiling water and boil until tender. Drain thoroughly, then transfer to a bowl. Mash until smooth, then leave to cool.

2 Grate the remaining potatoes and place them in a bowl of water for 15 minutes to draw off the starch.

3 Reserving the white starch that has collected at the bottom of the bowl, remove the grated potato and dry with a tea towel. Pour away the rest of the water.

4 Add the grated potato, starch and the remainder of the ingredients to the mashed potatoes, season with salt and pepper, then mix well until the ingredients come together to form a potato dough.

Green Potatoes

When potatoes turn green the tuber is highly toxic, equally the leaves should also not be eaten, as the potato plant is part of the deadly nightshade family. English gardener John Evelyn (1620–1706) advocated eating raw potatoes pickled as a salad, but people soon realised that a poor diet containing too many raw potatoes sometimes caused an eczema-like condition that was believed to be a form of leprosy: even as late as 1795 one David Davies was predicting that 'though the potato is an excellent root, deserving to be brought into general use, yet it seems not likely that the use of it should ever be normal in the country'.

➔ The best way to prepare a potato? Cook it.

YOU WILL NEED

- 500g potatoes, such as Nadine or Cara, peeled and quartered
- 100g self-raising flour
- 100g breadcrumbs
- 50g salted butter
- 1 tbsp chopped parsley
- a little grated nutmeg
- salt and pepper
- fried bacon lardons and onions, to serve (optional)

5 Piece by piece, break off enough dough to form rough, golf-ball-sized dumplings, pressing each one firmly so that it holds its shape. Add a little more flour if the mixture feels too wet and the dumplings fail to hold together.

6 Bring a pan of lightly salted water to a gentle simmer (don't let the water boil as it will cause the dumplings to fall apart). Gently drop in the balls, bring the water back to a simmer and cook for 15–20 minutes, until firm and cooked through.

7 Serve with fried bacon and onions, or as a potato substitute with any main dish. If you prefer, you can place the raw dumplings on the top of a nearly cooked stew, casserole or thick soup and simmer them until cooked that way. This will give them a lovely flavour.

Recipes from around the world
India

Brought to India by Portuguese traders the *aloo* made slow progress in that nation's cuisine. Until, that is, urban India boomed and its millennials began to demand more potato products.

Aloo Gobi

Use Charlotte or Jazzy potatoes for a firmer finish in this dish, or mashers and bashers such as King Edward for a more floury finish.

YOU WILL NEED
- 2 tbsp vegetable oil
- 1 tsp black mustard seed
- 1 onion, sliced
- 2 garlic cloves, chopped
- 1 tsp garam masala
- 1 tsp curry powder
- 1 tsp turmeric
- squeeze of tomato purée, or 200g fresh or tinned tomatoes
- 250g potatoes, peeled and diced small
- 250g cauliflower florets
- 110ml vegetable stock
- fresh parsley or coriander leaves, to garnish

1. Heat the vegetable oil in a large pan over a medium heat. Add the mustard seed, onion and garlic and fry until softened.
2. Add the garam masala, curry powder and turmeric and cook briefly.
3. Add the tomato purée or fresh or tinned tomatoes, then the potatoes and cauliflower florets, stirring to coat them in the spicy mixture. Cook the vegetables for a few minutes to allow them to absorb the flavours.
4. Add the vegetable stock and simmer slowly until the potatoes are cooked.
5. Serve garnished with fresh coriander or parsley leaves.

Bombay Potatoes

A dry dish, Bombay potatoes or Bombay *aloo*, goes well with *pudlas* or vegetable pancakes.

YOU WILL NEED

- 450g salad potatoes, such as Charlotte or Jazzy, chopped into equal-sized pieces
- 1 tsp turmeric
- 4 tbsp vegetable oil
- 1 dried red chilli
- 6 curry leaves
- 2 onions, chopped
- 2 green chillies, chopped
- 50g fresh coriander, chopped
- 1 ¾ tsp asafoetida
- 1 ½ tsp each of cumin, yellow mustard seed, fennel seed and nigella seed
- squeeze of lemon juice

1 Par-boil the potatoes in lightly salted water laced with the teaspoon of turmeric. Drain and set aside.

2 Heat the oil in a pan. Add the whole dried red chilli and the curry leaves and cook for 30 seconds.

3 Add the onion and remaining ingredients and cook until well softened.

4 Add the potatoes, turning them gently to coat in the spices. Cook on a low heat for 7 minutes, or until the potatoes are soft.

5 Remove the dried red chilli and curry leaves, then serve with a squeeze of lemon over the dish.

Recipes from around the world
Ireland

Ireland has a special relationship with the potato and celebrates it with a range of dishes made with several potato varieties – including the Lumper, the potato that failed during the great famine, but which is now making a comeback.

Boxty

Boxty, or potato cake, was the traditional dish for All Saints' or All Hallows' Day, generally celebrated on 1 November. It's a great winter-garden dish made with a mixture of cooked, mashed potato and raw grated potato, cooked on a griddle placed over a campfire. Tatti Scones are Scotland's equivalent of the Irish boxty. Same ingredients, same method, but a different name. You can prepare the cakes in advance and store them in the fridge until you're ready to cook – on a pan over an open fire is particularly authentic.

YOU WILL NEED

- 2 large spuds, such as Desirée or Lumper, peeled and grated
- 350g cold mashed potato
- 1 tsp salt
- 1 tsp bicarbonate of soda
- 2 tbsp plain flour

1 Place the grated raw potatoes on clean a tea towel or layers of kitchen paper, roll up and squeeze out the moisture with your hands.
2 In a mixing bowl, combine the grated tattie with the mashed potato and the salt.
3 Combine the bicarbonate of soda and the flour in a separate bowl, then add to the bowl with the potato mixture. Mix everything together to form a stiff dough.
4 Roll out the dough until 1cm thick, trim the edges and cut the dough into four equal squares, or form the mixture into pancake-sized rounds.
5 Heat a griddle or heavy-based frying pan over a high heat. Reduce the heat to medium and add the potato cake. Dry-fry for 15 minutes on each side, or until cooked through and golden all over.

Colcannon

Colcannon crops up across Ireland, the greens in the dish variously being provided by anything from cabbage to kale. Traditionally, cooks may add mashed parsnip or a bunch of spring onions along with a ring and a thimble. The diner who found the ring was sure to marry soon; the thimble finder would, perhaps sensibly, avoid the altar. A hedgerow version, served in spring and sometimes called Champ, substituted fresh nettle tops for greens. Adding cream in place of the butter gives a richer dish.

YOU WILL NEED

- 900g–1kg potatoes, such as Golden Wonder or King Edward
- generous helping of greens, such as a small Savoy spring cabbage, a handful of curly kale and leeks, chopped
- 250ml whole milk, heated until nearly boiling
- generous knob of butter
- salt and pepper

1   Scrub the spuds and cook them, in their skins, in a pan of lightly salted boiling water. When they are halfway done – 10 minutes or so – drain off two-thirds of the water, put a lid on the pan, turn off the heat and let the potatoes steam to finish cooking, until tender.
2   Meanwhile, in a separate pan, steam the greens until tender.
3   Slip the skins off the spuds, mash, season and add enough milk and butter to beat into a lovely, fluffy purée. Stir in the greens and serve.

'Did you ever eat colcannon
When 'twas made with yellow cream
And the kale and praties blended
Like a picture in a dream?'
Traditional verse

Recipes from around the world
Italy

Simple Italian cuisine, each dish often containing only three or four ingredients, has made its mark across the world, especially where pasta is concerned. Gnocchi was often served as a *Primo* or first course.

Gnocchi

Potato gnocchi (the word may come from their likeness to the knuckle, or *nocca*) are particular favourites in central and northern Italy. The key to keeping them light is to work with the potato when it's as hot as you can handle it.

YOU WILL NEED

- 300g floury potatoes, such as Estima or Maris Piper, diced
- 1 egg yolk
- 1 tsp olive oil
- 125g type '00' or plain flour
- 50g salted butter
- salt and pepper
- Parmesan cheese, to serve
- basil leaves, to garnish

Flavoured Gnocchi

You can flavour the gnocchi with a couple of teaspoons of pesto, which you should add to the dough before rolling and cutting.

1 Cook the potatoes in a pan of lightly salted boiling water until tender. Drain well, leave them to dry out a little, then mash.

2 Transfer the mashed potato to a floured chopping board. Make a well in the centre and add the egg yolk and olive oil, then season. Add the flour a little at a time, using a fork then your hands to bring everything together to a stiff dough.

3 Take a small section of the dough and roll it into a thin sausage shape on a floured work surface. Cut along the length of the strip to form small gnocchi. Using the back of a fork, press into the top of each dumpling to create a griddle effect. (This helps the gnocchi 'hold' the sauce.) Repeat until you have used up all the dough.

4 Cook the gnocchi in a pan of lightly salted boiling water. Keep the pan on a gentle, rolling boil and scoop out the gnocchi with a slotted spoon as they rise to the surface – about 3–5 minutes.

5 Transfer the gnocchi to a warmed serving dish and dot with butter. Sprinkle with Parmesan and serve garnished with basil leaves.

Recipes from around the world
Peru

With 500 years of multicultural history behind it, Peru has become renowned for its fusion foods, combining European staples with traditional produce such as quinoa, beans and *patatas*.

Salchipapas

This street food originated in the coastal city of Lima, now Peru's capital. It's a simple dish: fresh, fried chips combined with fried sliced *salchipapas*, or sausage, usually frankfurters. For a slightly healthier, home-made version, roast your own chips in the oven and add some good-quality frankfurters. Kids love this, for obvious reasons!

- 600g potatoes, halved
- 3 tbsp light olive oil
- 200g frankfurter sausages, sliced into bite-sized pieces
- 1 red onion, peeled and cut into wedges
- 3 or 4 tomatoes, cut into wedges
- salt and pepper
- tomato ketchup, mayo and mustard, to serve

1 Bring a pan of lightly salted water to the boil, add the potato and cook for 8–10 minutes, until beginning to soften. Drain and set aside.

2 Heat the oil in a roasting pan, then tip in the dry potatoes. Shake to coat the spuds with the hot oil and cook in the oven for about 30 minutes, until the potatoes are nearly cooked.

3 Meanwhile, fry the frankfurter pieces until they start to colour, add the onion wedges and cook for another 3–4 minutes. Add this mixture to the roasting tray of potatoes along with the tomatoes, stir through and return to the oven for another 5–10 minutes.

4 Transfer to a large serving platter, drizzle some mustard, mayo and ketchup over the top and serve while hot.

Recipes from around the world
Spain

The first Europeans to encounter the South American potato went on to incorporate the spud into a wide range of regional dishes back home.

Patatas Bravas

This tapas dish has become a favourite around the world. It is simply fried potatoes topped with a spicy tomato sauce, but somehow it becomes so much more than the sum of its parts.

YOU WILL NEED

- 350g new potatoes, such as Maris Bard or Lady Christl, peeled and cut into small chunks
- 3 tbsp olive oil
- ½ tsp cumin seed
- 1 onion, chopped
- 1 garlic clove, chopped
- 1 red chilli, seeded and finely sliced
- ½ tsp smoked paprika
- 400g tinned tomatoes
- salt and pepper

1 Place the potato chunks in a roasting tray, sprinkle with salt and mix in 2 tbsp olive oil. Add the cumin seeds. Roast in the oven for 40 minutes, until soft on the inside and crispy on the outside.

2 Meanwhile, heat the remaining olive oil in a heavy-based pan, add the onion and fry for 5–6 minutes. Add the garlic and chilli and fry until soft. Add the smoked paprika and the tomatoes, then season. Cook, covered, until the sauce is thickened. Keep warm.

3 Transfer the roasted potatoes to a warm serving dish. Reheat the tomato sauce, if necessary, and spoon over the potatoes. Serve straight away.

Tortilla

Simple, yet delicious, *tortilla de patatas* makes a perfect picnic or lunch dish.

YOU WILL NEED

- olive oil, for frying
- 400g waxy potatoes, such as Jazzy or Rocket, peeled and thinly sliced
- 8 eggs, beaten
- 1 large onion, sliced
- salt and pepper
- parsley leaves, to garnish

1 Heat a good slosh of olive oil in a deep frying pan, then add the potatoes. Cook, turning often so all the slices are cooked on both sides, and some are golden. This will take about 15 minutes. Transfer any pieces of potato that are cooked ahead of the rest to the bowl of beaten eggs.

2 Add the chopped onion to the pan when the potatoes are about halfway done. Keep cooking until the onions are translucent and all the potatoes are cooked. Tip everything into the beaten egg. Add a couple of large pinches of salt and some pepper and mix in gently.

3 Clean the pan and add a little more oil. Place on a medium heat. Pour in the egg and potato mixture and cook gently for 10 minutes, or until the base and edges are set and golden.

4 Place a plate on top of the pan and invert the tortilla on to the plate. Slide it back into the frying pan to cook on the other side, until set.

5 Serve the tortilla warm or cold, garnished with parsley leaves.

Recipes from around the world
Sweden

Like its Scandinavian neighbours, Sweden has a particular love for potatoes, especially when teamed up with fresh dill, as in *Gräslökstuvad potatis* – leftover new potatoes in a cream and dill sauce. However, it's probably their hassleback potatoes, a buttery version of roasties, that have travelled the world most successfully.

Hasselback Potatoes

Introduced by an inventive Swedish chef in the 1950s, hasselbacks make the perfect mid-season roasties or a Christmas Day special.

YOU WILL NEED
- 400g maincrop spuds, such as King Edward or Maris Piper; or 400g second earlies, such as Nadine or Kestrel
- 50g butter
- olive oil, for roasting
- sprigs of rosemary
- 2 garlic cloves
- salt and pepper

1. Slice into, but not through, each potato at 3mm intervals with a kitchen knife. (Stand the potato on a wooden spoon to stop yourself slicing it through.) Heat the oven to 180°C/350°F/Gas 4.
2. Melt the butter with the olive oil in a roasting tray. Carefully roll the potatoes in the oil and butter, then place them cut side up. Scatter over the rosemary, place the whole garlic cloves in the tray, and season well with salt and pepper.
3. Roast in the oven for around 1½ hours – you may need longer if the potatoes are large. The important thing is to baste them well every 10–15 minutes; it's this that gives them their gorgeous, golden, crispy finish.

Recipes from around the world
Switzerland

Rich dairy and cheese dishes combined with good, home-grown vegetables typify the Swiss country cookbook and potatoes feature in many regional dishes, such as *vaudois*, *raclette* and *fondue*.

Rösti

A national dish, the traditional home of rösti was on the German-speaking side of the *Röstigraben*, the 'rösti ditch' between the German- and French-speaking parts of Switzerland. You can lighten up these simple potato cakes with grated celeriac or other root vegetables. You will need a 10cm stainless-steel cutter or food ring to make the rösti.

YOU WILL NEED
- 2 generous-sized potatoes, such as Kind Edward or Majestic
- duck fat or vegetable oil, for frying
- salt and pepper
- smoked salmon and sour cream, or a fried egg, to serve

1 Grate the potatoes and thoroughly squeeze them dry in a kitchen towel or colander. Divide the grated potatoes into four equal portions.

2 Melt the duck fat or heat a good glug of oil in a frying pan. Place the cutter in the centre of the pan and fill it with one portion of rosti, pressing down the potatoes carefully with the back of a spoon. Remove the ring and repeat to form the other three rösti.

3 Cook for 3–4 minutes, until golden, then carefully turn over to cook the other side.

4 Eat with smoked salmon and a dollop of sour cream, or for breakfast with a fried egg.

Recipes from around the world
USA

Good American cuisine is a wonderful combination of round-the-world recipes and home-grown ingredients. It's also the continental home of the potato, which naturally features on every diner menu.

Hash Browns

A hearty breakfast staple, which owes a debt of gratitude to the Swiss rösti, hash browns are great served with bacon and eggs.

YOU WILL NEED

- 450g grated raw potato, liquid squeezed out
- 1 onion, chopped and lightly cooked
- 4 tbsp vegetable oil, for frying
- salt and pepper
- parsley, chives or chervil, to garnish
- 4 fried eggs, to serve

1 Mix the grated potato with the cooked onion and season with salt and pepper.
2 Heat the oil in a heavy-based pan over a medium–high heat and, when hot, spoon the potato mixture into a thick pancake-shaped disc in the middle of the pan.
3 Reduce the heat and allow to cook, pressing down on the hash brown with a heatproof spatula from time to time, and tidying up the edges, until the underside is brown.
4 Flip the hash brown over, or turn with the spatula, and cook the other side until brown.
5 Cut into four and serve hot, topped with a fried egg.

Travel Food

'Twas laying in the platter
Sure something just immense.
Served with a spoon and butter
And it only costs ten cents.'
Northern Pacific advertising jingle

If the baked potato is one of our most nutritious and accessible street foods, it created a runaway advertising promotion for one US railway company. The Great Big Baked Potato became the mainstay of the Northern Pacific Railway (NPR) after one of its dining car managers overheard two farmers bemoaning the fact that they could not sell their oversized potatoes. He bought the lot and the NPR promoted the Big Spud meal for decades.

Potatoes even made it into outer space after astronauts aboard the 1995 Space Shuttle Columbia experimented with growing seed potatoes. The expectation is that on long-distance space journeys the spud will not only provide food and water, but also clean the air, removing excess carbon dioxide and replacing it with life-giving oxygen. Space technology, meanwhile, is coming to the aid of Earth-bound farmers. Satellite data is to provide early warnings of crop diseases, allowing farmers to target treatment more efficiently.

⬇ Space Life Science-1 (SLS-1), launched aboard Space Shuttle Orbiter Columbia on 5 June 1995, was the first Spacelab.

Potato Drinks

Eat drink and be merry. This versatile vegetable can be brewed into a beer, distilled to make a craft vodka or, for a healthy choice, supped solo.

Making Potato Beer

There was a time when potato beer would have been greeted with scorn and derision. However, decades of bland, characterless, aerated ales – and the meteoric rise of the craft-beer brewer – has put home-brewed potato beer back on the menu.

Potatoes were regularly added to the brewer's mash during the 1940s, when Britain was running short of grain during

⬇ Potato beer: a welcome addition to the craft of beer making.

⬆ 100% pure potato juice, which is very rich in potassium.

World War II. These days, you can use spuds in the form of potato flakes; as mashed, unpeeled, but well-washed spuds; or washed, peeled and grated. Some brewers prefer a mealy, floury spud; others swear by earlies. But does potato beer really taste of potatoes? Some insist their brew lacks the spuddy flavour, while others promise a subtle, but distinct tuber aroma.

↑ The domestic still had become a rarity in Ireland by the 1900s.

Home brewing is a craft. The brewer has to be scrupulously clean, masterful with their yeasts and hop flavours, and creative when it comes to naming: one German beer was called *Kartoffelferien*, after the school 'potato vacation'.

Potato Plus Four

As well as potatoes, home-brewed beers require four essential ingredients:

- grain in some form
- water
- yeast
- hops to flavour the brew

Our recipe also includes brewing sugar to produce a second fermentation in the bottle and finings that help clear the beer; potato beers can be cloudy.

Potato Beer

This makes 22.5 litres or 45 pints. Ensure you thoroughly sterilise the fermenting bin, muslin bag and bottles before using.

YOU WILL NEED

- 1kg potatoes, washed and cubed
- 100g hops, such as Fuggles or East Kent Goldings
- 1.5g crystal malt
- 2.5kg crushed pale malt
- 1 sachet top-fermenting beer yeast
- 1 sachet of beer finings
- 125g brewing sugar

1 Boil the potatoes until they are tender. Drain, reserving the potato water, and mash the potatoes. Place the mash in a muslin bag.

2 Put the hops, the muslin bag of potato and the two malts in 5 litres of water and 'mash' for an hour at 60°C/140°F.

3 Remove the potatoes, squeezing out as much of the liquid as possible and add the hops. Bring the mash back to the boil, then leave to cool.

4 Transfer to the fermenting vessel through a filter, add the yeast and 22.5 litres of cold water. Cover this, called the wort, and leave to ferment for a week.

5 Seal with a lid and an airlock and leave for a further 10 days.

6 Add the finings to clear the beer, then rack it off into a clean, sterilised bin.

7 Add the sugar, dissolving it first in a little warm water. Siphon the beer into bottles and leave for four weeks before sampling.

Simple as One, Two, Three

The beer will go through three basic stages of brewing, each requiring a particular piece of kit:

1 The mash: nothing to do with mashing the spuds, this mash involves steeping the grain and potatoes in water and bringing the mixture to the boil. Depending on the quantity of beer you plan to make, a large, stainless-steel pan (the kettle of the professional brewer) should suffice. The alternative is a purpose-made, stainless-steel, self-heating – and expensive – boiler.

2 The wort: this is the liquid drawn off from the mash, which will be transferred to another vessel to ferment. This fermenting bin is a relatively cheap plastic bin with a sealable plain lid. An improved version includes an airlock at the top and a tap at the base.

3 The bottling: finally, the brewer needs to bottle the beer into glass vessels. Bottles can be bought with bottle tops or fitted with reusable swing-top lids fitted with a rubber seal.

Eau de Vie

You can distil, or purify, any fermented drink from any field crop. The result, usually a clear liquid, is what the French call *l'eau de vie*, 'the water of life'. The business of making eau de vie is an art: Irish monks, who brought home the craft of distilling grains from their devotional journeys to the Holy Lands almost 1,500 years ago called the resulting liquid *uisce beatha*, 'the water of life'. Their tongue-tied masters, who could not pronounce the Gaelic, called it whiskey.

Every culture has its own: apple-based calvados in Normandy, rum-based Newfi screech in Newfoundland, rice sake in Japan. The potato, too, was distilled to make alcohol both in its Peruvian homeland and its adopted Irish home, where the alcohol was known as poitín or potsheen. In Scandinavia, it was aquavit (although made from both potatoes and grains); and in Russia – and Britain – there was potato vodka and gin.

The backyard boozers that produced these eaux de vie were never popular with authorities and, as happened during the American Prohibition, they were gradually outlawed, leaving licensed producers cornering the market and bringing in tax revenues. During the 1830s in Ireland, the temperance movement of Father Theobald Mathew took a heavy toll on country stills (almost half the adult population signed a pledge of alcoholic abstinence), while the potato famine saw most of the country's estimated 2,000 licensed distilleries and countless secret country stills shut down. By the early 1900s no more than 30 survived. Recipes were lost or forgotten and poitín was eventually legalised in

← These Irish poteen makers were on the wrong side of the law when the *Picture Post* photographer came to call in 1952.

Ireland, but not Northern Ireland, only in the late 1990s.

The act of distillation is simple enough and although the web is full of explicit directions on how to produce your own eau de vie, unlicensed distilling is illegal.

Yet, like craft beers and lagers, craft eaux de vie are enjoying a revival. William Chase, a Herefordshire farmer who started out making crisps, moved into licensed potato vodka and gin production. Growing old-fashioned, high-starch varieties, such as Lady Claire and Lady Rosetta, on his farm, he set up a plant to mash, ferment, distil and rectify the spuds. The resulting

↑ From potato field to bottle on one site: the Chase Distillery in Herefordshire is the brainchild of William Chase, who started out with the craft crisp, Tyrell's, before moving into potato-based eau de vies including vodka, above, being hand bottled on the farm, and gin.

high-octane eau de vie was then diluted down to a 40% vodka with water from a local aquifer. The same vodka served as a base sprit for the farmer's gin, flavoured with juniper and other botanicals. As he put it, 'The reason my vodkas and gins were special was because we made everything from our Herefordshire potatoes.'

'My gin … is without doubt the best thing that I've ever made from potatoes.'
William Chase, *One Potato, Two – Finding the Magic*, 2015

Midsummer Potato Wine

This delightful wine takes a year to mature. Start it in late June with the last of the second earlies and uncork the first bottle on midsummer night the following year. You'll need a large pan, a couple of demijohns with airlocks, and six wine bottles.

YOU WILL NEED

- 3kg potatoes, cleaned and sliced (skin on)
- 1.2kg brown sugar
- 2 litres white grape juice
- 200ml cold tea
- 1 sachet wine yeast mixed in a little water
- 1 Campden tablet

1 Put the potatoes in a pan with enough water to just cover them. Bring to the boil and simmer until tender. Strain the liquid into a fresh pan and discard the potatoes.

2 Add the sugar to the potato water and heat gently until the sugar has dissolved.

3 Let the syrup cool a little, pour it into the demijohn and add the grape juice, cold tea and enough boiled – not boiling – water so the yeast brings the liquid level up to the shoulder of the demijohn.

4 Fit the airlock and leave in a warm place to ferment for 24 hours, then move to a cooler position out of direct sunlight and allow to ferment for 10–12 more days.

5 Rack off the wine into a second sterilised demijohn and leave for a week to settle. Repeat two or three times, racking the wine off each time into a clean, sterilised demijohn – the starchiness in the potatoes takes a while to clear – before adding a Campden tablet to clear the wine, and finally bottling into sterilised bottles and labelling.

Index